To Neal Worshaw —
Best,
Danny May

W9-BEY-439

To my fellow Canceroids, their families, loved ones, and friends… to everyone whose life has been touched or scarred by cancer— I lovingly dedicate this tale to you. It is my sincere hope that you find a welcome measure of comfort in my words and stories… the equivalent of a warm, compassionate hug from a kindred spirit.

≈≈≈≈≈

Within these pages I claim at least a partial understanding of science. That being said, absolutely nothing between these covers should be construed as qualified medical advice, nutritional advice, or any other sort of health-related advice in lieu of that of a competent, duly licensed physician. For that matter, I strongly suggest that you don't even attempt to follow my recipes for any important dinner parties without practicing them first.

≈≈≈≈≈

Everything presented as factual in this book represents the best of my ability to accurately recall the details of real events and diligently research scientific and historical sources. I apologize in advance for any unintentional errors printed herein. A few names have been changed or abbreviated in order to protect the privacy of certain individuals.

≈≈≈≈≈

The affliction that befell me has been variously known as "Hodgkin's Disease," "Hodgkin's Lymphoma," and other names. In accordance with the most recent literature and the World Health Organization Classification, I have chosen to use the term "Hodgkin Lymphoma."

≈≈≈≈≈

Back cover photo from Danny and Andrea's wedding by Dale LaDue.

1

CHEMO HONEYMOON

OYSTERS FOR ANDREA

JANUARY 6, 2008

Remember your most powerful teenage crush, the one that changed the way you walked and dressed and even breathed? Unrequited (or so you might have believed) it never completely went away; rather, it permeated and skewed your perception of potential partners through college, marriage, and beyond... gone forever, he or she seemed, and yet permanently engraved into your subconsciousness.

Now try to imagine suddenly having the chance to enjoy a cozy dinner together, just the two of you, after thirty years of separation.

Andrea was two years behind me in school, but we were even closer than that in age. I first took notice of her when she was an eighth-grader, trying to cajole her way past the faculty chaperones and into our high school dance. The bewitching sparkle in her gemlike, blue-gray eyes instantly made me a little crazy... possessed by the notion of her companionship, insanely jealous at the thought of her with anyone else. Although young Andrea wasn't your standard-issue looker, she was nonetheless a strikingly beautiful young teenager— tall and thin, with elegantly sculpted features seemingly lifted directly from ancient Rome.

Andrea was no bouncy, big-chested cheerleader; rather, she was a unique and exquisite work of the Almighty Creator's art, perfectly beautiful without artificial adornment. I *had* to claim her, somehow capture her attention as she began her freshman year a few months later. But how possibly could I? In our high school's prevailing jock-ocracy I had counted for very little. Though I would later blossom into something of a self-made athlete— a karate black belt, a competitive rower, and football-less Wayne Central's first NCAA gridiron starter— this was hardly

3

apparent in my scrawny, 160-pound build back then. I've always been a late bloomer.

I suffered like this throughout my high school junior year. Finally, emboldened by the encouragement of a sympathetic senior a few doors down, I mustered the courage to ask Andrea out to a movie double-date in the summer of 1975. We shared a perfunctory but sweet kiss upon her doorstep at evening's end, leaving me incapable of sleep. It was hard to tell, but I think she liked me a little. However, several of Wayne Central's smooth-talking athletic types were on to her, I soon learned, and I would surely lose out to one of the more popular guys before long. Feeling desperate to continue holding her attention as the fall semester of my senior year began, I accordingly thought nothing at the time of borrowing a car from a friend— unlicensed though I was— and taking Andrea out for another date.

We went to see Roman Polanski's "Chinatown," and then to a diner for late night tea. We cuddled a little more cozily as I dropped her off, and then on my way home I took a curve too fast and proceeded to roll my soon-to-be-ex-friend's Pontiac twice sideways and once lengthwise at approximately highway speed. During one of these horrifying revolutions I was thrown through the opening whence the passenger door had been shorn. Somehow, I walked away with only a broken wrist and a few scratches after the smoking wreck came to rest on the other side of the road in our town judge's front yard. Miraculously alive, I was nonetheless stone dead as far as Andrea's mother was concerned. She authoritatively suggested that a more experienced driver would be a preferable beau for her beautiful young daughter.

Halfway through college I moved back to my native Massachusetts. Years and then decades passed, but my infatuation with Andrea remained in the back of my mind. I would most likely never see her again, I figured, and so I would try to make peace with the indelible etching of her within my skull. For the most part I succeeded. But then, many years later, we actually did get back in touch.

When the "information superhighway" opened to public traffic in 1994, it enabled e-mail, e-commerce, e-porn, e-everything between consenting adults. It also afforded high school alumni from my era a perfect way to reconnect— snail-mail was too much work and perhaps seemed to my generation somewhat old-fashioned, while phoning someone out of the blue after many years might have come off as inappropriately abrupt, or maybe just plain weird. But when a graduate of little Wayne Central High School of Ontario, New York took the initiative to launch an alumni website, I enthusiastically signed up and started e-mailing old friends. Andrea, however, wasn't there, at least not yet. I would wait... like a patient stargazer hoping to spy an expected comet (or, given my rural boyhood, like a hunter in a tree stand) I would wait for her.

"Remember me?" I shyly wrote her, heart in throat, when she finally materialized a couple of years later.

For six years Andrea and I regularly corresponded across our three hundred mile separation. We had both been married and divorced, and we were also both running our own businesses. Additionally, we were each in long-term relationships with our respective business partners, and so our communications were appropriately benign, though, in retrospect, loaded with powerful, unspoken feelings. I kept Andrea abreast of all of the dynamic changes in my professional and personal life, and she in turn provided spiritual guidance and pithy counsel, advice smarter and wiser than my preconceived expectations of her. And then, late in 2007, Andrea suddenly announced to everyone on her e-mailing list that her life had suddenly changed, that she would thenceforth be a solo act.

As inexorably as winter yields to spring's vernal reawakening, long-dormant longings suddenly fluttered within my chest in response to Andrea's new "available" status. I immediately sensed in my heart and my gut what I needed to do— I would drive five hours each way in order to cook dinner for her, a get-together rife with explosive possibilities and yet without any pre-discussed ground rules or parameters. If nothing else, this was going to be interesting. We arranged this unlikely rendezvous for the first Sunday in January. Andrea and I agreed that it would be a belated Thanksgiving dinner, a feast that she had been unable to enjoy on the usual day because of her overwhelmingly demanding work schedule.

Without the need of my alarm clock I excitedly arose at 3:00AM on January 6, 2008. A tropical air mass, most unusual for January, was in the process of melting all of the early winter snow as I drove west through upstate New York toward the small town of my childhood. As the sun peeped over the eastern horizon directly behind me, spring-like warmth wafted through my little Hyundai's open windows, the unseasonably balmy updrafts further elevating, it seemed, my already soaring heart. As is typical of me I arrived well ahead of schedule. I'm never late for anything, especially something as important as this.

With a built-in hour to kill, I managed an invigorating workout at the Penfield, New York YCMA. This was a cost-free session, graciously volunteered by the Y's desk clerk after I convinced her that I was a reigning indoor rowing champion from out of town, hoping to employ their facility for my morning exertions in preparation for my next big race. Creative canard though it might have been, it was not really all that far from the truth.

Andrea was still in the shower when I finally located her driveway. I found my way inside and waited for her at her kitchen table, nervously occupying myself with a cluster of grapes from her fruit-bowl. As I did so it struck me that we hadn't actually seen each other in person since the disco era. Might one or both of us be shocked by the other's timeworn appearance? My mind's eye unsentimentally aged her thirty hard years, as if to prepare me for the worst. But Andrea looked exquisitely lovely and many, many years younger than her age as she descended her staircase still barefoot, her eyes a-sparkle as ever and the rest of her every bit as gorgeous as I remembered. For her part, she easily recognized me. After a tentative hug and some slightly awkward small talk, it was time to get cooking, I declared.

Our January Thanksgiving dinner would feature the traditional fare, albeit gluten-free in deference to Andrea's dietary requirements. Flour is relatively easy to avoid at Thanksgiving, I explained as I sliced and chopped. One might opt for a rice-based stuffing, and perhaps thicken the gravy with cornstarch or even pureed vegetables. As the turkey slowly roasted we would enjoy a small, quick repast and then take the proverbial "long walk on the beach" along Lake Ontario's unseasonably warm shore.

I knew that this first dish was crucial, as it would set the tone for the rest of our day together… and, perhaps, our future.

"Care for some eggs?" I nonchalantly suggested. The "eggs," such as they were, would actually serve as the precious ornamentation that elevated this oyster creation to a higher plane.

The quote "'Twas a brave man who first ate an oyster" is variously attributed to Mark Twain, Jonathan Swift, and Sir Walter Raleigh. However, in spite of the oyster's uninviting, geologic exterior, it has been consumed and greatly appreciated for several millennia, well before any of these men were born. In the modern culinary era, the oyster has come to occupy a special page in the European and American repertoires, often betokening opulence or a grand occasion, not unlike champagne. "Oysters Rockefeller," for example, is the gastronomic manifestation of nineteenth-century robber baron wealth, an icon of late-1800's luxurious extravagance. And whether or not oysters can physically cause romantic arousal, as is often alleged, they are generally regarded as sexy food. The legendary lover Casanova was known to down twelve *dozen* before his main course.

But I wasn't necessarily trying to bedazzle Andrea with culinary wizardry, nor was I attempting to bio-chemically seduce her right there over the dinner table. Rather, my intention was to prepare a dish that would be poignantly emblematic of our reunion— as elegant as Andrea's features; rich and soul-satisfying, but not excessively indulgent. And it would have to be relatively easy to prepare, or at least easy *looking*, for no one enjoys a meal that seems to have entailed considerable suffering. The pressure was on. But having spent the majority of our thirty-year hiatus in fine restaurant kitchens, I was up to the challenge. My dish for this occasion would be the updated version of Oysters Rockefeller that I once put on the menu of a French restaurant that I had managed right after college.

I placed six fresh and deliciously briny Duxbury Bay oysters in a small saucepan with just enough boiling water to steam them open while leeks braised in a separate pan. As soon as the oysters cracked their smiles, I set them aside. From the reduced, oyster-enriched broth I whisked up a buttery cream sauce in which I then wilted leaves of spinach. As with the

7

classic version of Oysters Rockefeller, a drop of Pernod liqueur would have been most welcome.

Then came the reconstruction— I spooned creamed spinach into the empty oyster shells, which I had kept warm in the oven; I swirled the leeks and oysters in the sauce and then positioned them atop the spinach; I added a little more sauce, and then, finally, those "eggs," generous spoonfuls of American sturgeon caviar. (Not as indulgent as it might seem— half-price after New Year's, just $20 per two-ounce jar.) It was a delectable combination.

After scooping the last of the caviar and cream from our shells, our lakeside stroll revealed, among other things, that my thirty-three-year infatuation with Andrea had been far more reciprocal than I had ever realized. I had been her first "real" date as well as her first kiss, she told me as we walked, squeezing our warm hands together as sparks steadily flew. Much to my surprise, I had been in the back of her mind in one form or another for all of these years as well. Nature's apparently intended course unfolded quite rapidly during those delicious afternoon hours, as if we were picking up right where we had left off as two young teenagers, albeit with the benefit of our decades of accumulated wisdom. We both clearly sensed right away how all of this would go.

The ensuing week was a blur of manic excitement and sleeplessness. Like a total coward I broke off by e-mail my part-time dating relationship with the terrific Manhattan redhead I had been seeing on recent weekends. I vaguely blamed myself for what I suddenly claimed to see as our "irreconcilable socio-economic incompatibility." It was an indirect and fancy way of admitting that I couldn't afford her Big Apple tastes much longer, which was actually true. Andrea and I talked and cooed by phone for hours on end every day, often in the middle of the night, and dozens of text messages flew back and forth.

Barely a month into our newfound bliss, Andrea energetically collaborated with me to assemble and host "Danny May's First Annual Super Bowl Eve Charity Wine Tasting." A year before, I had raised a healthy pile of money for the Cardinal Hayes Home for Children by soliciting sponsorship for my indoor rowing races. But for some reason I didn't feel quite up to competing as the calendar flipped to January of 2008.

Andrea and I attracted a small but enthusiastic crowd, and the tasting was both successful and fun. My boss's well-heeled and elegantly dressed entourage included a renowned Hollywood comedian. Williams College Head Football Coach Michael Whalen lent the event his charisma and *gravitas* to accompany his knowledgeable insights into the next day's Patriots-Giants game that all of us would be watching. In return for his generous assistance, I promised to help out at his annual summer football camp.

We managed to cut another substantial check to Cardinal Hayes in spite of the rapidly souring economy. All of our attendees seemed to have gotten their money's worth; none of them, I'm sure, had any inkling that Andrea and I were already secretly engaged.

Less than a week after our reunion dinner, Andrea had showed up on my Great Barrington doorstep at five o'clock in the morning. That Sunday night we enjoyed a glass of wine at a swank little restaurant on my block. Although it was just our fifth date, strictly speaking, right there at Allium's cozy little bar Andrea abruptly asked me to marry her. Of course she knew I'd assent, mainly because I was incapable of saying no to her. We immediately began to prepare for a mid-September wedding, which would coincide exactly with the thirty-third anniversary of our disastrous third date. The days of the week even coincided.

After what we thought might pass for a decent enough interval so as not to appear rash or foolish, we excitedly told Andrea's friends, her family, and then mine. Everyone seemed genuinely thrilled. My immediate future— OUR future— loomed like blindingly bright and warm sunshine above the horizon with nary a cloud in sight. We were giddily and yet securely in love, the kind of gooshy, juvenile love that silly songs and bad movies are written about... the kind of love that otherwise reasonable people desperately spend their lives and their fortunes hoping to find.

And then on the afternoon of Friday, March 28, I found a strange new lump in my neck.

SOMETHING MISSING, SOMETHING WRONG

Andrea's sudden entrance into my atmosphere from her safely distant orbit in cyberspace had come just as I was beginning to sense a vague emptiness in my life. A year and a half earlier, in the summer of 2006, I had walked away from my half of a restaurant and gourmet food and wine business, departing with only my accumulated cooking knowledge and a laptop computer to show for my decade of toil. Both would soon come in handy as I re-entered the "real world."

A man who can knowledgably cook and write need not be independently wealthy in order to enjoy the company of brainy and beautiful women, I soon learned. With my more normal, post-restaurant work schedule, I was suddenly free to emerge at last from my post-divorce funk and explore the world of on-line dating and its intriguing possibilities. My romantic safari took me to the pillows of a rock-climbing engineer-geek, two professional psychologists, an accomplished classical musician, and an especially gorgeous computer executive whose razor intellect rendered invalid every blonde joke. Like a perfect fool, I regularly sent Andrea— who by then had evolved into my on-line, platonic "spiritual advisor"— a steady stream of e-mails describing all of these affairs in exquisite biological detail. My keeping her thus informed was, in retrospect, an indication of the zero probability I had ascribed to the prospect of ever revisiting our brief high school romance.

Finally, in the autumn of 2007, I started seeing Rachel, a pizzazzy, redheaded Manhattan magazine executive. We were having lots of fun, I excitedly reported to Andrea. But something was missing... something was wrong, I faintly sensed as winter's weak morning light began to peep through the curtains of Rachel's rural Connecticut bedroom on the first morning of 2008. New Year's day was to many people a time of renewal, a day for them to begin keeping their resolutions, which, if they stayed the course, would make them better people and enrich their lives, blah, blah, blah.

But rather than renewed, I felt numb that morning— numb not from a night of New Year's revelry, but rather from the preceding fortnight of brutal holiday work shifts at Guido's Fresh Marketplace, the gourmet grocery store where I doubled as the wine manager and the seafood department prep cook. Though not as demanding as the restaurant world I had recently escaped, the Guido's workload predictably got heavy around holidays. New Year's Eve itself had been the toughest shift of all, a second consecutive twelve-hour day of hoisting heavy pots of boiling water for cooking case after case of shrimp, and then hundreds of pounds of ice for chilling them. My entire skeleton ached.

I had quickly cleaned up after work and arrived at Rachel's little paradise of a weekend getaway home around 9:00PM on December 31… ready, I thought, to ring in the New Year with champagne and style. Rachel normally had the energy of a sugared-up pre-teen, but she was tired, too. We aimlessly fumbled around the kitchen, unable to recapture the rhythm that had been so productive for our dinner parties over the past few weekends. It may or not have been midnight already when we collapsed into bed, too tired for anything but sleep.

Rachel was a fabulous catch by any standard— intelligent, successful, and very pretty, with a keen palate for food and drink honed in restaurants in Manhattan and around the world. A decade before, she and I would never have crossed paths. But our worlds had recently intersected on an Internet dating site. Rachel was interested in meeting men near her new Connecticut weekend home; I, in turn, had been willing to travel an hour or more away from my Great Barrington apartment in order to meet women like her.

We had immediately clicked on our first date. Upon donning an apron in Rachel's exquisitely remodeled country kitchen that October Sunday, my years of professional cooking experience dovetailed deliciously with her zest for entertaining. After surprisingly awaking together the following morning, I drove her to the Wassaic train station, parting for our very separate worlds while eagerly looking forward, we agreed, to our next weekend together.

It was ten weekends later that we dithered through New Year's Day, our mutual exhaustion overwhelming everything from our enthusiasm for our half-planned dinner party to our eye-to-hand coordination. Even our ability to speak seemed impaired. Jerilyn, Rachel's Connecticut housemate, dropped in and out, as did several other of their Manhattan friends with weekend homes nearby. The holiday ticked by in formlessness, with no real dinner plans materializing as several bottles of champagne seemingly emptied themselves without human effort.

A couple of tear-jerking, chick-flick DVDs had Rachel softly sobbing beside me on her sofa for most of the afternoon. But then she and Jerilyn seemed quite taken aback when the ending of the second feature aroused in me a powerful flashback to a similar situation from my youth, a vivid and bittersweet recollection of my father that suddenly had me moist of eye as well. From there the conversation turned to antidepressants.

I explained to Rachel and Jerilyn that as a general rule I avoided dating women who regularly used such medication… certainly not because I condemned those who battled chronic depression, God bless them, but because such drugs were so over-prescribed. Of course we all have our ups and downs, and yet there is often wisdom and even beauty to be found in the depths of life's natural cycles. Absent an actual diagnosis of clinical depression, to pharmaceutically annihilate this aspect of one's experience, I suggested, was perhaps to miss out on opportunities for personal growth. Some of the most interesting people I've ever met had survived deep troughs of despair and self-doubt, only to emerge stronger and smarter.

But I've been on Prozac for twenty years," shrugged Rachel. "It's been great for me…" Jerilyn nodded in apparent concurrence.

And so went my New Year's Day of 2008. The afternoon's lengthening shadows reposed like felled timber across my path back to Massachusetts the next day as I pondered several imminent little changes in my life. My shorter winter work hours would allow me more time to spend at the gym on my beloved rowing machine, I promised myself. Also, I had enrolled in a modest retirement plan beginning in 2008— just enough, really, to afford a proper headstone when my time came, but at least it was a start. My health insurance through my job would also kick in, and with that I would treat myself to a thorough (and long overdue) physical examination when I could get around to it.

As 2008 dawned I had a newfound measure of security, and I had Rachel. I should have been pleased with my circumstances. However, something was missing, something was wrong… but what? Was my relatively recent emancipation from the tyranny of eighty-hour-a-week restaurant work affording me, ultimately, only the time for these haunting misgivings? The opportunity to behold occasional glimpses into the actual emptiness of my existence?

Rachel and I had agreed that the first weekend after New Year's would be a rare "off" week for us. Some especially Orthodox friends would be visiting, she apologetically explained, and my clearly non-Jewish presence would be as awkward as that of her Connecticut Christmas tree, which would likewise be removed for the occasion. And so, with a slightly uneasy conscience, I offhandedly informed her that I would be filling this void in my schedule by innocently meeting up for lunch with an old acquaintance— oh, yes, a female— whom I had not actually seen in person since high school.

* * * * * * * *

Nearly three months into 2008, I was working, as usual, behind the seafood counter at Guido's when my right hand's fingers suddenly wandered upon the painless, rubbery lump above my left collarbone. *"What the fuck is THIS?"* I immediately blurted to my boss Michael, who was standing nearby. It was Friday, March 28… a date I shall never forget.

The painless, coin-sized mass just above my collarbone was unlike any swollen gland I've ever had. Unlike those one associates with colds or allergies, it visibly protruded from my neck, as if I had swallowed a ball bearing. Why hadn't I noticed it before? Had it really come on so quickly without me feeling it? I found it impossible not to wonder whether it might be somehow related, on some cosmic or supernatural level, to my newfound joy with Andrea. Could this mysterious health-issue-in-the-making be its grand, karmic counterbalance? God Almighty's idea of a "good news/ bad news" joke?

Andrea's presence was required in Rochester for most of the winter and spring of 2008. Because of a contract foul-up, she needed to cram a year's worth of her environmental education programs into six months. And when not performing for her audiences of charmingly enthralled schoolchildren as "Greta Garbage," she was spending as much time as possible with her ailing, ninety-three year-old grandmother.

Andrea arrived in Massachusetts the day after I found my lump, and she joyfully conducted— without compensation— a wine tasting at Guido's simply to afford us more time together. Between our sickeningly loving glances across the seafood counter, my hand kept pondering my left clavicle for clues. Might it be an infection of some sort? A lymphatic reaction to my recent filling replacement? My mother the nurse practitioner would know what to do. Andrea and I would be seeing her the next day, as we had planned a family get-together that weekend at my sister's home in nearby Saratoga, New York.

"It's probably nothing serious," my mother Mary unconvincingly suggested as I prepared our dinner on that first Sunday after Easter, even as the color drained from her features. I could tell that she was secretly horrified, that this was in fact a potentially serious matter. "But *do* get in to see your doctor!" she repeated several times throughout the afternoon.

Although I've rarely done so, on this occasion I immediately took Mary's advice. Early Monday morning I called East Mountain Medical Associates ("EMMA") in Great Barrington. Dr. Andrew Potler, D.O., my primary physician, was unavailable on such short notice, as one would reasonably expect. However, a Physician's Assistant named Neal W. would be able to see me that same day.

Physician's Assistants have grown in number in recent years. During such an office visit they pretty much do everything the actual doctor would, except make the tough calls that a doctor's degree (and his malpractice insurance) are intended to cover. Mr. W. took an aggressive, workman-like approach to my situation, almost as if I were a car making an unfamiliar rattle and he, the mechanic, knew exactly how to run the standard factory diagnostics.

"Yes… it *could* be an infection," Mr. W. half-heartedly agreed. But it could also be any number of things, including lymph cancer, or something called sarcoidosis, a barely-understood autoimmune disease often characterized by chronic inflammation of the lymph nodes. Whatever the final diagnosis, he assured me with a dismissive wave of his hand, it was readily treatable. He ordered a chest x-ray for me the very next day in nearby Fairview Hospital, which made me wonder— might this Mr. W. be treading upon Dr. Potler's turf to some degree? I wasn't quite sure how office politics worked in a medical organization like EMMA.

The x-ray, explained Mr. W., would surely prove useless, but it was a necessary dance-step to get my insurer ("HMO Blue") to pay for a CT ("computed tomography") scan. On my way to Fairview's radiology department I ran into Dr. Potler in the hospital's hallway and quickly brought him up to date. Without hesitation he reached out and groped my neck with hands seemingly endowed with some sort of natural power, the divine gift to both diagnose and cure that separated true healers from mere medical professionals. I sensed that Dr. Potler knew right then a little more than he could prudently tell me.

The chest x-ray, as expected, revealed nothing, and so I went in for a CT-scan of my neck two days later.

* * * * * * * *

The surgeon's scalpel has long been a necessary tool in the diagnosis and treatment of many internal disorders. Until just a few years ago, for instance, medical assessment of a new cancer patient's lymph system required a surgical procedure that would allow direct examination of the regions above and below the patient's diaphragm for tumors. But this operation— the "staging laparotomy"— has been rendered largely obsolete in modern medical practice. The relatively recent marriage of existing x-ray technology and new-fangled computer science afforded doctors the opportunity to take a three-dimensional image of a patient's internal organs, viewable like a tour through the torso as the hundreds of x-ray "slices" meld into a cinematic continuum. Thus the product of a CT-scan is known in medical jargon as a "study" rather than an "image," as with a static x-ray. Should the CT-scan study reveal cancerous lymph nodes, then state-of-the-art combination chemotherapy further obviated the need for surgical intrusion by effectively seeking out and destroying such malignant cells throughout the body wherever they might be hiding.

The CT-scan, though far less invasive than exploratory surgery, is considerably more involved than a mere chest x-ray. It exposes the recipient to approximately four hundred times the radiation, and an intravenously administered chemical formulation is necessary to facilitate visual contrast. This CT-scan contrast injection comes with bizarre side effects— a metallic taste in the mouth, and a sensation of wetting one's pants. Reactions to this substance, when they occur, are quite strong. Furthermore, a CT-scan of the full torso, should I eventually need it, would entail the prior ingestion of a second contrasting substance to line my digestive tract.

The only thing redeemingly cool about a CT-scan, other than its priceless diagnostic value, of course, is the circumstances of its origin. Credit for its invention is due not only to the joint Nobel Prize honorees Sir Godfrey Hounsfield and Allan McLeod Cormack, but also, perhaps, to John Lennon and Paul McCartney. In the 1960's, Capital Records was a division of Electric & Musical Industries Ltd., or EMI. Thanks to Beatlemania, the lush profits from Capital's strong record sales afforded EMI's Central Research Laboratories, where Hounsfield worked, the means to develop CT-scan technology.

Shortly after arriving for my appointment, I was escorted from the radiology desk to the CT-scan room. The technicians positioned me on a gurney-like surface that would slide me through a large, donut-shaped device as it rapidly snapped x-rays and then sent them to the main computer. Before starting, they made the usual inquiries about allergies and medications, and then warned me again about the intravenous contrast. I would first get a test dose; should I suddenly exhibit the rarely seen, "Exorcist"-like reaction to it, they had a special rescue cart with the necessary antidotes on hand. Their proximity to the hospital's emergency room, they privately admitted, was not a coincidence.

Though certainly scary, it was less so than the possibility of having cancer that was slowly creeping into my consciousness.

Thanks to high-speed Internet traffic, my CT-scan results were available to Neal W. in hours rather than days. He phoned me himself at Guido's that same afternoon to immediately discuss— IN PERSON!— its findings. I'll be equally pissed and relieved, I thought at the time, if it turns out that I had missed two hours of work and driven forty miles just to hear something that he could have easily told me over the phone.

No such luck.

The CT-scan of my neck had confirmed what my own fingers had already learned, that I had a swollen lymph node. However, there was also visible in the study's lower periphery a cluster of additional swollen lymph nodes in my chest. Something was indeed quite wrong with me. Neal W. narrowed the likely diagnoses to either sarcoidosis or some type of lymph cancer. I finally asked whether Dr. Potler was in the loop on this. Sensing my unease, Mr. W. immediately reached out into EMMA's hallway and pulled my primary physician into the examination room.

Dr. Potler was uncharacteristically adamant. "We need to get ON this!" he said. "NOW!"

In other words, I was probably in for a long and difficult battle... a challenge without precedent in my life thus far, and something that I might not necessarily survive.

Testing...

As Andrea shuttled between Rochester and the Berkshires most weekends, my April of 2008 was largely devoted to a lengthy sequence of medical tests and procedures. The "Computer Tomography" evidence of swollen lymph nodes in my chest had necessitated a second, full torso CT-scan less than a week after my first. But this time it would be slightly more complicated, for I would be required to drink twenty-four ounces of contrast, the equivalent of a full bottle of wine.

To my professional *sommelier*'s palate, the barium sulfate contrast solution ("READI-CAT®") was a repulsive concoction; so much so that, going forward, it would become the low benchmark by which I assessed the worst of the wine samples proffered by my salesmen. Considerably thicker than milk and chalky in texture, it had a strong if flavorless presence in my mouth. And yet it had no acidic grip, no progression of familiar fruit or floral nuances that remotely suggested what we wine mavens call "drinkability." My poor tongue, accustomed to swirling the great Chardonnays and Rieslings of the world, repeatedly twitched with involuntary spasms, as if to expel it as one's body might reject an alien organ. While willing myself to swallow it, no food pairings sprang to mind, and I would definitely recommend to my fellow end-users a very low serving temperature... if for no other purpose than to thoroughly numb one's taste buds.

After all of that unpleasantness, the full torso CT-scan itself was a piece of cake. It clearly confirmed the presence of additional "lymph node involvement," a cluster of abnormal growths in my mediastinum, the area behind my sternum. Now we had to find out exactly what the hell they were. Since it was highly likely that the comparatively accessible lump in my neck was directly related to the masses deep within my ribcage, Neal W. referred me to the offices of Sharon Ear, Nose, and Throat, conveniently located in the same building as EMMA. There Dr. Ari Namon would take over the case.

A needle biopsy of the lump above my collarbone, explained Dr. Namon, was a relatively quick and easy office procedure. All he would need to do was plunge a fat needle deep into my lower neck as I sat before him fully awake, and then he would withdraw a tissue sample of sufficient size to examine microscopically and thereby reach a definitive diagnosis. If I was ready, he could do it right then and there, he volunteered.

Dear reader, be it known at this point in my tale that I absolutely hate looking at needles intended for human flesh. I hate the sight, color, smell, and even the thought of blood; and I especially don't enjoy the smorgasbord of pains commonly associated with the practice of medicine or dentistry. However, at critical times such as this, my experience as a competitive indoor rower comes to my rescue and serves to distinguish me, at least to some degree, from mankind's multitudes of cowardly, jelly-boned wimps.

* * * * * * * *

The sport of rowing dates to the seventeenth century. London's Thames River was by then a bustling nexus of commerce, and businessmen of that era frequently required livery service from one riverbank to the other. The most common mode of transportation across the Thames was the low-slung "wherry boat," powered by the oar-strokes of a "waterman," as its pilot was known. Races between off-duty wherry boats naturally arose, and thus competitive rowing was born. However, lest I mislead anyone, I have only rowed an actual boat in real water exactly twice. The sport of "indoor rowing" takes place atop the exercise machines on which competitive rowers train all winter.

To the physicist, the *erg* is a unit of work, expressed in scientific units as force times distance. But to the ears of a collegiate rower, "erg" is short for the Concept2 Rowing Ergometer, my exercise machine of choice. Collegiate rowing programs have since the late 1800's strived to devise exercises to facilitate effective winter training, and numerous incarnations of mechanical rowing machines have been manufactured over the last century. In 1981, a pair of Vermont oar-manufacturing brothers patented their newly-invented Concept2, a refreshingly inexpensive and portable rowing simulator. Their early improvements included an electronic performance monitor so accurate that it was finally possible for rowers around the world to meaningfully compare erg times.

It wasn't long before a Boston-based club consisting of former collegiate rowers (The C.R.A.S.H.-B's, for "Charles River All-Star Has-Beens") decided to hold erg races in order to add a little humor to their arduous winter regimen. The event has since grown many-fold and has morphed into the World Indoor Rowing Championships, drawing thousands of serious competitors from around the world to Boston every February. Dozens of other erg races fill out the indoor rowing calendar all winter, and their colorful names reflect this sport's fundamentally masochistic nature. The Great Baltimore Burn, the Mid-Winter Meltdown, the Tough Love Indoor Rowing Championships, and, naturally, the St. Valentine's Day Massacre are but four well-known races held within weeks of the C.R.A.S.H.-B. races.

Serious ergometer training for such events is alternately mind-numbingly boring (long, aerobic segments) and brutally painful (short anaerobic intervals) with little obvious reward beyond the tremendous cardiovascular benefits and the sculpture of one's ass into a pair of hard, round cannonballs. Former collegiate rowers tend to regard this contraption as medieval non-believers once viewed the rack— as a dreaded torture device. The erg races themselves are so hellishly painful as to constitute a spiritual rite of passage, not unlike those among Earth's most primitive cultures as described to us by anthropologists. Many an ex-oarsman has likely endured gum surgery or other similarly intricate office procedures simply by reminding himself during his interminable hour in the chair that at least he wasn't on an erg.

And this is how, as veteran of many hundreds of hours of painful ergometer training as well as a few medal-worthy races, I was going to endure Dr. Namon's needle biopsy.

* * * * * * * * *

Dr. Namon seated me in something like a dentist's chair, and then anesthetized the skin above the lump in my neck with a topical balm. I averted my eyes as he drew forth the needle, visualizing myself instead rowing through a ten-thousand-meter training piece… hovering just below my aerobic threshold as the concomitant flood of endorphins pulsated through my vessels. Rowing like this, though indeed strenuous and boring, can also be, in some strange way, somewhat meditative. Before I knew it the procedure was over. Now came the waiting, as histological analysis of the tissue would definitely take longer than it did to receive the results of the CT-scans. Andrea and I spent even more time on the phone than usual.

My mother, bless her seventy-six year-old heart, has devoted more than half a century to caring for the sick, the injured, and, most recently, the addicted. In the early 1950's, as health care professionals of her generation were just beginning their careers, they understood that medicine had little to offer the cancer patient beyond mere pain relief. Death was nearly automatic. Such a notion, especially when absorbed by youthfully impressionable ears as medical scripture, can be stubbornly difficult to displace. As if to permanently embed this truism in my mother's fresh young mind, a month before her eighteenth birthday she was assigned to a surgical floor filled with hopeless and dying cancer patients.

It was understandable, then, that my mother saw little wiggle room between my illness and what she had long understood to be its inevitable outcome. "It already is whatever it is," I replied in response to her offer of support in the form of prayer as I awaited my test results. "We just have to find out, and then deal with whatever I have."

"Wow…" she replied in seemingly awestruck amazement. "How quickly you've gone through all of the stages. Right to… *acceptance*!"

While it might make sense at some later juncture in my case to invoke Elizabeth Kübler-Ross and the step-by-step process of dying with which she is so closely identified, I reminded my dear mother that it was still just a little premature to think of me as terminally ill.

"Inconclusive, but suspicious," was Dr. Namon's verdict a few days later, over the phone as I worked at the counter at Guido's. Suspicious of what? Sarcoidosis was still alive as a possible diagnosis, a fading sliver of hope that I did not in fact have cancer. "Not sarcoidosis..." continued Dr. Namon, "the— the *other thing.*" But because the results of his excavation into my neck tissue were less than definitive, a full surgical biopsy would be the next step, he explained. At this precise moment I was struck by the realization that I most likely had cancer... but what kind? Was I going to be dead sometime soon, as my mother seemed to believe?

A week later Andrea accompanied me as I checked into the day surgery ward at Fairview Hospital. Three hours later I checked out without my swollen lymph node. Dr. Namon had completely removed it, secretly knowing damn well, I strongly suspected, that it was cancerous just by looking at it. Furthermore, he had needed to do some intricate knife and needle work, severing and then reconnecting a lymph duct. While I was still under anesthesia, Dr. Namon explained to Andrea that I was forbidden to lift anything heavy (such as a wine box) for the next five days so that his surgical artistry could heal properly. By the time I came to, Andrea had apprised everyone on my cell phone's contact list— including one of my old girlfriends— of my status.

As I regained my senses I was relieved to be without the lump. Whether it was cancerous or not, it had been an unwelcome intruder, something foreign to my body. Now all we could do was wait for the definitive assessment. As we did, I delved into on-line medical research, which drove us both a little crazy. If in fact I had cancer, it was probably some form of lymphoma. Only one-sixth of all lymphoma cases are of the eminently treatable Hodgkin variety. The other five-sixths, loosely categorized together as non-Hodgkin Lymphoma, came in about forty different types and ranged from chronic, untreatable annoyances to acute and life-threatening diseases.

"Be careful what you wish for," we've been sagely counseled through the ages. That being said, if one must have cancer, then Hodgkin Lymphoma is perhaps the cancer you want. As I recovered from my surgery, Andrea and I were left with little to do but hope and wonder for seventy-two hours— sarcoidosis, or cancer? If cancer, then Hodgkin or non-Hodgkin? We discussed all of the possible outcomes, including even my death. And we talked about our wedding plans.

"Please don't answer me right away," I asked Andrea at one point. "I want you to give this some serious thought…" I suggested that we get married *before* the treatments began, as I dreaded the thought of forever seeing myself frail and debilitated from chemotherapy in our wedding pictures.

But more importantly, I explained, I had begun to believe that everything unfolding between us was part of some beautiful, divine plan. I had overcome extraordinary odds to emerge relatively unscathed from that awful car crash in high school. We had then found our way back to each other after three decades and across three hundred miles. And now that we were about to entwine our paths forever, I was suddenly facing the most serious health issue of my life. I knew that this challenge would be many times more bearable with Andrea beside me as my wife, my soul mate, my partner, and my confidant… all of this because we had been somehow pre-ordained for these roles in each other's lives.

Since the earliest hours of our remarkable reunion back in early January, Andrea and I had found it ridiculously easy to pour out our feelings to each other directly from our hearts. It was immediately apparent as we snuggled on her sofa that magical January afternoon that we were powerfully drawn toward each other, that our togetherness was destiny… and that any hesitation to move down the hall and dive between her linens was rapidly dissolving. Unbelievably, perhaps, I was the reluctant one, afraid that immediately consummating our obviously mutual urges might actually do Andrea and our nascent relationship more harm than good. I had already waited— rather patiently, I'd say— a third of a century for her. She, in turn, was only a couple of months out of a long-term relationship that had emotionally and physically drained her. I didn't want to mess this up.

But perhaps physical intimacy might contribute to her healing process, she had protested, declaring somewhat out of the blue, "I want to be one of your lovers!"

"Andrea," I immediately replied, savoring as they rolled from my tongue the words I had always wanted to tell her, "You are the ONE... I love you; I've always loved you, like I've never been able to love anyone else... I love you too much to have you be just *one of my lovers*." If we were to cross this threshold, I knew, it would have to be permanent, for I couldn't bring myself to contemplate a life after Andrea.

And now, just four months later, Andrea and I were morbidly discussing, theoretically, her life after I died. "I'll move to the celibate wing of the *ashram*," she insisted.

"Bull—SHIT!" I snorted. "You need to love and be loved way too much for that... and besides, you're WAY too gorgeous! You'll hook up with someone else in no time." A month or so after I croak, I playfully predicted, Andrea might well awaken within the arms of her new boyfriend to an unexpectedly deep snowfall.... as the wheels of his snow-bound vehicle spin in her driveway, Andrea will unsentimentally grab the urn-ful of my ashes and say, "Here! Pour some of this crap under your tires..."

"Well," giggled Andrea, "maybe I won't necessarily remain *alone* forever... but I'll NEVER remarry! Whatever happens, I'm going to my grave as your wife, MRS. MAY."

* * * * * * * *

Three days after the surgery, Dr. Namon phoned me with the results as Andrea and I passed the time with one of our increasingly frequent scenic drives around the region.

"How sure are you about this?" I eagerly asked.

"I'm giving you these results with one hundred percent certainty. The lab results were very clear."

"Thank you." Thus did I learn that I had joined the illustrious club of Hodgkin Lymphoma patients that included the Pittsburgh hockey great Mario Lemieux, his Pennsylvania Senator Arlen Specter, Microsoft co-founder Paul Allen, and the late Los Angeles Rams' owner Daniel Reeves, who had perished from the disease in 1971. Dr. Namon wished me luck and referred me to a local oncologist named Dr. Michael DeLeo for further treatment.

"Anyone else available?" I asked. "I mean, is he the only one in the area?" I like being able to choose such things for myself.

"We refer *all* of our patients to Dr. DeLeo," replied Dr. Namon matter-of-factly and without hesitation. Hmmm... this DeLeo guy must have the whole county rigged, I figured. Either that, or he's pretty good.

Under the circumstances, we had just received the best news possible. As we drove around our tri-state region that afternoon, Andrea and I had both of our cell phones fully engaged, simultaneously calling all of our friends and relatives right away to tell them. That night we celebrated our wonderful fortune with a bottle of *Brut Rosé*— pink champagne, my favorite type of wine in the world, and something I've been sharing with Andrea from time to time as I gradually exposed her to my universe of liquid treasures. It was now late April, and I estimated that my chemotherapy treatments would probably begin sometime in late May. Might we actually be married by then? Although the idea seemed unreal, it was nonetheless an immensely satisfying notion.

I fell asleep that night content and secure in Andrea's arms. However, I awoke the next morning to the harsh realization that I in fact had cancer, and that it was actively trying to kill me.

Time moves slowly for newly diagnosed cancer patients. Doctor's appointments are usually separated by weeks rather than days, as if there were no particular urgency to attack and defeat this inner enemy. Most cancers do in fact progress at a glacial pace. While certain rare malignancies sweep through the body like a September wildfire, many others smolder symptomlessly for years before being detected. A month delay between my diagnosis and my first actual treatment would be of no significance, I reminded myself a few times.

Word of my condition quickly spread around my workplace. A week or so later I was tenderly approached by "Reenie," the eighty-year-old widow of the late Guido Masiero himself. In a tone hushed and somber with sympathy she half-whispered, "*I hear you have a problem…*"

"No…" I replied in my calmest, most reassuring voice, "I don't have a problem; *cancer* has a problem!" Cancer, I confidently assured this lovable old sweetheart, was in for the worst summer of its life.

* * * * * * * * *

I had *cancer*, I kept reminding myself. CANCER! One of the harshest words in the English language… maybe because of the phonetic contrast between the hard and soft "C's." The first akin to the shatter of cold glass, the second like a jagged shard's swift slice through one's soft, unsuspecting flesh… almost like the shock of such a diagnosis, followed by its body-ravaging treatment. "*KAN-sur.*" No… the words "courtesy" and "concert" share a similar progression of sounds without any such connotations. Perhaps the word "cancer" so jars the ear because it has long been synonymous with a death sentence… and not as in an instantly lethal jolt of voltage or a mercifully swift drop through a trap door, but rather a long and agonizing ordeal through which the vital forces incrementally, irreversibly ebb from one's being until the grim reaper's bony knock, at long last, is gratefully welcomed.

There was a time not all that long ago when one dared not utter the word "cancer" in polite company, like the Victorian-era taboo against words like "pregnant" and anything else suggesting that humans actually procreated. One never *died from cancer,* per se. One *passed away after a lengthy illness,* usually behind closed doors and beyond the sight of children and all but the closest relatives. However, my generation grew up in front of our television sets, and we were thus able to watch such famous stars as Rod Serling, Chuck Connors, and Desi Arnaz literally smoke themselves to death right in our living rooms.

Smoking had become synonymous with cancer beginning in the 1960's, and accordingly the dreaded "c-word" entered more regular usage right around then. Medical science, meanwhile, was finally making progress upon cancer's uniformly dismal prognosis during that tumultuous decade. Improved diagnostics (such as the CT-scan) made cancer more detectable in its early stages. Beams of radiation could be used to kill malignant tumors deep within the body, as could intravenously administered chemical compounds. For the first time, the medical community was beginning to speak with guarded optimism about "survival rates."

And the cancer that above all others had demonstrated that the disease was survivable, that it was not an automatic death sentence, was the malady first definitively identified by British physician Thomas Hodgkin in 1832.

THE CANCER YOU WANT

So what exactly is this thing called cancer, this monstrous malady responsible for one in six deaths worldwide? Might it be one of nature's fundamental self-limiting mechanisms, some sort of built-in time bomb that eventually kills off us humans if nothing else does so first? Hard-wired within our cells to make them suddenly turn bad upon some mysterious signal? Compared to the long roster of infectious diseases conquered by modern medicine, cancer might well seem like mankind's most stubborn adversary. Although it was identifiable to the ancient Greeks and Egyptians, medical science had lacked the wherewithal to make a noticeable dent in cancer's carnage until the twentieth century, when atoms became divisible, surgery reliably antiseptic, and the biochemistry of DNA understood.

Like the beings whose organs they comprise, human tissue cells are born, reproduce, and then die, a finite life cycle that is part of their innate programming. Indeed, we humans are completely refurbished, cell-by-cell, every seven years or so. But when something goes particularly awry on the molecular-genetic level, cells don't die when they should and continue not only living but also reproducing. The resulting surplus of cells leads to the development of a tumor, a life form unto itself, in some ways, with its own powerful will to survive, an independent, animal-like intelligence. Determined to perpetuate itself and multiply, a cancerous tumor will crowd out or destroy healthy tissue and even spread its cells to other organs in the body, as a wildflower scatters its fertile seeds to faraway fields.

But cancer, though a prolific slayer over the centuries, is not completely invulnerable to counter-attack. In order for cancer cells to be so deadly, it follows that they must be different in some way— and thus discernable— from healthy tissue. Any cure, then, would ideally exploit this difference. For example, chemotherapy drugs, poisonous as they are, are even more toxic to fast-reproducing cells such as those of a malignant tumor than to healthy, slower-dividing cells. Likewise, the ability of cancerous cells to rapidly multiply comes at the expense of their capacity to mend themselves when damaged, as normal cells can. High-energy wavelengths of ionizing radiation, therefore, can be used to incapacitate cancer cells beyond repair without permanently destroying nearby healthy tissue.

Many an earnest grade-schooler or well-coached beauty contestant has expressed a desire to "find a cure for cancer," as if there lay hidden somewhere a single magical substance awaiting discovery. But just as there are many very different types of tissue in the human body, there are a wide variety of human cancers. It is not necessarily accurate to collectively identify them with a single word, or to attack all of them the same way, as their characteristics vary so widely. Some cancers form solid tumors, others not; some immediately betray their presence with obvious outward symptoms, while others lie camouflaged for years within the body. And many types of cancer are still today nearly one hundred percent lethal, but it is my extraordinarily good fortune that the malignancy I would have to face and conquer was Hodgkin Lymphoma, also known by its initials HL.

* * * * * * * *

The lymphatic system is one of those human body components of which few of us, I suppose, ever become aware unless something goes wrong with it. In terms oversimplified enough to understand myself, here's how it works—

This network of ducts and almond-sized nodes, part of the human body's immune system, carry lymph fluid, which contains white blood cells. These cells, known as lymphocytes, identify and attack a variety of infectious and abnormal cells, including those that appear to be

29

suspiciously cancerous. There are two major subtypes of lymphocytes: B cells and T cells. The B cells produce antibodies, proteins that circulate through the blood and lymph fluid and "tag" their quarry. The T cells, thus alerted, identify and kill them. Afterwards, some of the B and T cells "remember" the invading pathogen and are thus able to fight it off should it return. It is a special irony that the human lymph system, which wages a constant battle against cancerous cells, can itself develop cancer... kind of like a three-alarm blaze erupting at the fire station itself.

Lymphoma is the general term for perhaps forty different cancers, including HL, that originate in the lymph system. HL is distinguished from the others by especially large and readily observable characteristic cells, as well as the unusually orderly progression of symptoms from one lymph node to its immediate neighbor. The other lymphomas, though collectively categorized as Non-Hodgkin Lymphoma, cover a wide spectrum of sub-types. With both HL and Non-HL, malignant lymphocytes are able to travel to neighboring lymph nodes (and remote organs) via the lymphatic ducts, just as a band of thieves might surreptitiously navigate an art museum though its ventilation network. It is worth noting that while several other types of cancer similarly utilize the lymph system to metastasize throughout the body, they do not transform into lymphoma by doing so. Cancers of all types retain their original identity even as they migrate to other organs.

Hodgkin Lymphoma was likely the disease first identified by the Italian physician Marcello Malpighi in his 1666 treatise *De Viscerum Structura Exercitatio Anatomica.* However, it was named for the British physician Dr. Thomas Hodgkin (1798-1866) who identified a handful of cases in the early 1800's. Much of what was taught at European universities in Hodgkin's era, including medicine, was still rooted in classical antiquity. For instance, Hodgkin and his contemporaries were schooled in the primitive Hippocratic notion that the foundation of sound health was a proper balance of the four "bodily humors"— yellow bile, black bile, phlegm, and blood.

Considering his times, Dr. Hodgkin offered some especially modern-sounding advice on public health. Fully a century before the American Medical Association's reluctant recognition of the relationship between diet and well-being, Dr. Hodgkin warned of the dangers of excessive cream and butter; he argued in favor of whole wheat and fiber in the diet; he advocated the consumption of less sugar and meats while increasing one's intake of vegetables; and he cautioned against tobacco and alcohol.

In his position as the "inspector of the dead" and the perhaps even more ghoulish-sounding "curator of the museum" at Guy's Hospital in London, Dr. Hodgkin had the opportunity to explore the relationship between clinically observed illnesses and post-mortem samples of actual pathologic material. In particular, his examinations of enlarged lymph nodes in several similar cases inspired him to author the 1832 article, *On Some Morbid Appearances of the Absorbent Glands and Spleen*. It was Dr. Hodgkin who first recognized that this disease progressed from one lymph node to others, and that the spleen tended to become involved in the later stages of the disease. While reading his actual words, one might well recall that Hodgkin wrote this seminal treatise during the literary flowering of Hawthorne and Longfellow, and therefore we might forgive the vivid extravagance of his descriptive prose—

> ...There was extensive recent inflammation of the peritoneum, in the cavity of which there was a copious sero-purulent effusion, and the viscera were universally overlayed with a very soft light yellow coagulum, too feeble to effect their union, though evidently having a tendency to do so. The mucous membrane of the stomach and intestines was generally pale and of its ordinary appearance, but in some few spots it was softened and readily separated itself from the subjacent coat. The contents of the intestines were copious and of an unhealthy character, overcharged with bile. The mesenteric glands were generally enlarged, but one or two very considerably so, equalling in size a pigeon's egg, of semi-cartilaginous hardness and streaked with black matter. The substance of the liver was generally natural, but contained a few tubercles somewhat larger than peas, white, semi-cartilaginous, and of an uneven surface...

(Hodgkin, Medico-Chirurgical Transactions, 17, 1832, p. 70)

Although Dr. Hodgkin made these observations of morbid tissue without the benefit of a microscope, nearly a century later (in 1926) the Philadelphia pathologist Dr. Herbert Fox confirmed microscopically that two of Dr. Hodgkin's original three patients actually did have HL, while the other was found to have lymphosarcoma, one of the Non-Hodgkin Lymphoma sub-types.

Shortly before Hodgkin's death, Dr. Samuel Wilks of Guy's Hospital published an article in which he acknowledged Dr. Hodgkin's previous accomplishments. In it, Dr. Wilks coined the eponym "Hodgkin's Disease," correctly surmising as well that it was in fact a form of cancer. However, in the 1860's there was still no microscopically observed, cell-based description of the disorder. Finally, in 1872, the German pathologist Theodor Langhans succeeded in identifying the especially large cells that had been found to be invariably associated with the disease. Independently of each other, the German physician Carl Sternberg (1898) and the American Dorothy Reed (1902) formulated detailed descriptions of what eventually became known as "Reed-Sternberg cells," whose presence in biopsied tissue remains an important diagnostic indicator of HL. Following this important discovery, half a century passed before the first medically sound suggestion that the disease was curable. In the meantime, the unfortunate patients diagnosed with HL nearly always died from it.

As with many other cancers, death by Hodgkin Lymphoma often comes indirectly. The disease steadily weakens the body's immune system as it progresses, making the patient increasingly susceptible to other maladies and infections. In advanced stages, however, the HL patient is likely to find his upper lymph nodes so heavily swollen that they exert pressure upon the trachea as well as the main oxygen-carrying arteries... enough, even, to asphyxiate the patient as he sleeps.

The cure for HL was hardly an instantaneous discovery. Radiation, in the form of x-rays, was known to shrink tumors as early as 1901. But radiation could *cause* cancer as easily as cure it, and it would be many decades before the mysterious power of the inner atom was securely enlisted in battle against the disease. And as nuclear science was beginning to address various cancers with increasing effectiveness in the mid-twentieth century, biochemically-based treatment was simultaneously showing therapeutic promise. It stands today as one of medical science's most uncanny coincidences that these two very different anti-HL weapons— chemotherapy and radiotherapy— evolved along uncannily similar timelines. One might think of this as akin to separate mountaineering parties attempting Mount Everest from opposite directions, only to summit weeks later within the same hour.

Chemotherapy had enjoyed a pronounced head start over radiation, as mankind's knowledge of reactions between atoms long preceded any comprehension of interactions within their nuclei. Scientists have long sought cures for our pains and illnesses from among various plant and mineral extracts, from vitamin C to penicillin, from skin-soothing petroleum jelly to talcum powder. But medicine's optimistic reach often exceeded science's sound grasp, and there was frequently scant distinction between one's medicine and another's poison. For example, many nineteenth-century patients who had used arsenic for a variety of ailments wound up poisoning themselves to death. And yet in 1894 the British physician Sir William Osler observed that a particularly toxic formulation of arsenic ("Fowler's Solution") afforded temporary relief from Hodgkin Lymphoma. An actual cure was still many decades away, but Dr. Osler— the patriarch, perhaps, of chemotherapy— might well merit partial credit for identifying a possible cancer treatment among the laboratory's shelf of powerful poisons.

Any honest discussion of twentieth-century poisons would rightly mention mustard gas, by most accounts the cruelest weapon of the First World War. Rarely lethal, it nonetheless incapacitated troops by causing severe blistering of the skin and, when inhaled, the lungs. A couple of decades later, in the middle of World War II, the American liberty ship SS *John Harvey* was carrying a secret stockpile of nitrogen mustard (the next generation of such weaponry) when she was bombed at port in Bari, Italy. The explosions, which killed hundreds of troops and civilians, filled the immediate vicinity with a high concentration of aerosolized nitrogen mustard. Upon examining surviving victims, United States Army medical personnel observed reduced lymphocyte levels as well as general suppression of their lymphatic systems. Might derivatives of this horrible chemical weapon be worth testing as a therapeutic medicine for Hodgkin

Lymphoma? Thus was the possibility of anti-cancer chemotherapy raised anew, and an era of rapid experimentation and discovery ensued.

Single chemotherapy drugs, such as the Mechlorethamine derived from the nitrogen mustard, proved only temporarily effective against Hodgkin Lymphoma. But eventually doctors began to administer several different such drugs concurrently and thereby greatly increase survival rates. By the mid-1950's, the chemists were close to a cure for HL. So too were the nuclear physicists.

X-ray radiation was identified as a possibly useful weapon against cancerous tumors shortly after its discovery by the German physicist Wilhelm Conrad Roentgen in 1895. However, the most vexing aspect of radiotherapy was and continues to be collateral damage to healthy tissue. The relatively low-energy rays emitted by Roentgen's first crude x-ray tubes caused considerable harm to the skin and outermost body tissue, just as a bullet does the greatest amount of physical damage to that which most decelerates it. The gradual development of increasingly powerful and precise radiation-emitting equipment eventually enabled radio-oncologists to reach and destroy tumors just about anywhere in the human body. Their experience in treating Hodgkin Lymphoma patients also taught them to irradiate lymph nodes beyond the site of the actual tumors.

By the mid-1960's, practitioners of both radiotherapy and combination chemotherapy could jointly and independently of each other claim to have developed a cure for Hodgkin Lymphoma— in theory, at least, if not always in practice. Standard oncological protocols were in their infancy, and doctors were still engaging in trial-and-error. In 1970, when a routine chest x-ray for bronchitis revealed a suspicious shadow in the mediastinum of Barbara F., a thirty-five year-old New Yorker, patients were still often dying from the disease. Ms. F.'s laparotomy assessed her as Stage IIIA Hodgkin Lymphoma, and she appeared to go into remission after undergoing extensive radiation with no chemotherapy. In 1976, however, the disease reappeared as Stage IV, and Ms. F. underwent six months of chemotherapy.

In 1986, twenty-one year-old Janit S., a multi-sport collegiate athlete, fractured her pelvis in a bicycling accident. During her subsequent series of examinations she was diagnosed with Hodgkin Lymphoma Stage IIA, and Ms. S. was given the choice of chemotherapy or radiation. Having personally observed a number physically devastated chemo patients, and also hoping to have children someday, she chose the latter. During her treatments she was able to continue training for a 1987 series of triathalons despite the debilitating side effects of her radiation.

Like me, my Great Barrington neighbor Kathy R. will remember forever the exact time and place whereupon she suddenly discovered her swollen, telltale lymph gland. Ms. R. began chemotherapy treatments for her Stage IV Hodgkin Lymphoma in 1992. When she responded to the initial chemotherapeutic regimen with convulsions and pneumonia, her doctor switched her to a different, more recently developed protocol. But with the end of her chemo treatments in sight, Ms. R. abruptly cancelled her remaining infusions. She sought instead to achieve her cure via healthy changes in her diet, along with injections of a substance that was widely dismissed by the mainstream medical establishment as untested and based on faulty science.

Right over the state border from Great Barrington, Albert V. of nearby Columbia County, New York was diagnosed with Hodgkin Lymphoma in 1994 as his mother was concurrently battling lung cancer. During his six months of chemotherapy, Mr. V. suffered from extreme nausea despite the newly developed medication he had been given specifically to counteract it. He also went completely bald. Upon spying a pedestrian sporting a handsome-looking "doo-rag" about his hairless head, Mr. V. immediately ordered two from a sympathetic seamstress who refused to accept payment for them— one brightly-patterned for everyday use, and another conservative enough to wear to his mother's funeral.

At the conclusion of his chemotherapy treatments, Mr. V.'s doctors were divided— one suggested follow-up radiation, while the other thought it unnecessary. Four years later, Mr. V. realized that he and his doctors should have erred on the side of caution. The disease had returned, manifesting its presence as a swollen lymph node on his neck. This time around, Mr. V. was treated with a relatively mild chemotherapy regimen followed by localized radiation. By 1998, the two different therapies thus used in concert had become accepted as both more effective and less debilitating than the exclusive use of one or the other.

And so, like my Berkshire neighbors and fellow Hodgkin Lymphoma patients Barbara F., Janit S., Kathy R., and Albert V. before me, I was about to enter into the treatment that was necessary to save my life. Compared to them, however, I was better positioned to enjoy the fruits of medical history, experience that by the spring of 2008 had made the disease 95% curable and its treatment a well-established routine. There was just one huge and as yet unanswered question…

Where would I be treated?

THE ACE

Professional baseball clubs carry as many as a dozen pitchers on their twenty-five-man rosters. Like a rock-and-roll album packed with a mixture of catchy singles, covers, and forgettable filler, the Major League pitching staff is typically a heterogeneous lot— some specialize in starting games, others in finishing them; some occasionally do both, and still others do neither.

But on every staff there is one special starting pitcher, a proven winner who has repeatedly demonstrated his pitching mastery against top-level competition. This pitcher takes the mound for Opening Day and starts as many games as possible in the post-season. In between, over the course of the long summer, his fans and teammates expect him to win much more often than not. Despite such pressure, he shoulders his role with a rare balance of outward self-confidence and the underlying talent to justify it.

This pitcher is known as The Ace.

* * * * * * * *

"Are you going to Boston?" I believe it was a Guido's customer or two who posed this question during the days after I made my diagnosis publicly known. But soon enough my friends and family joined the refrain. "You'll get a second opinion, right?" And "If I were you I'd get myself right down to Dana-Farber!" From hearing all of this, one might have concluded that our Berkshire area oncologists did little but fill coffins for a living. The Boston idea, however, had its merits.

As a great American metropolis, Boston is rather small— only 600,000 call the city itself home. Boston and its immediate suburbs comprise

America's tenth-largest metropolitan area, as populous as Norway or New Zealand, and yet far, far behind New York, Los Angeles, and other "major" cities.

But Boston is second to none of them in many diverse areas of accomplishment. Beantown sports teams are regularly crowned world champions, and fine museums and restaurants abound. The Boston Symphony Orchestra (whose musicians I regularly fed during their annual summertime residency in the Berkshires) is considered one of America's "Big Five" ensembles. Most importantly of all, perhaps, the Boston area's concentration of world-renowned universities and colleges is without equal anywhere in the world. In the shadows of ivy-cloaked Harvard, Boston University, and MIT, one rightly expects to find cutting-edge technology-based businesses, like those clustered along Greater Boston's Route 128, "America's Technology Highway." One also finds excellent hospitals.

Massachusetts General Hospital, Beth Israel Deaconess Medical Center, and Brigham and Women's Hospital have long been national leaders in medical care and innovation. In addition, Boston's Dana-Farber Cancer Institute, an affiliate of Harvard Medical School, is, like the Boston Symphony Orchestra, among America's top five in its field as ranked by U.S. News & World Report. As a corollary of its status as a world-class cancer hospital, Dana-Farber is in the "second opinion" business, as patients from New England's outlying, small-city clinics and hospitals routinely seek their counsel.

But Boston was over two hours away from me. Undergoing treatments or even seeking consultation at Dana-Farber would have entailed missing full days of work, even for simple office visits. I couldn't realistically afford that. However, Dr. DeLeo and his Berkshire Hematology & Oncology practice (BHO) maintained an office near my Great Barrington apartment, and also one right around the corner from Guido's in Pittsfield.

Now, I had made a point of purchasing my Hyundai Accent from the dealership directly across the street from Guido's... not to avail myself of their shameless sticker prices or their rude customer service, but rather because I could theoretically drop it off for a brake job or some such repair without losing any time from work, a convenience that might well save me hundreds of dollars every year. But a life-threatening disease was a little more serious than a squeaky rotor… could I trust my life to Dr. DeLeo and Berkshire Hematology & Oncology? Should I "get right down to Boston" for a second opinion, if only to silence the throaty chorus of concern?

Most fortuitously, just as I was pondering these questions I again ran into Dr. Potler outside of his usual workplace. As if on cue, he appeared on the other side of the counter from me at Guido's, where we actually enjoyed more leisurely conversations than during our tightly scheduled office appointments at EMMA. I asked him about oncology care in general in our area, as so many people had obliquely hinted that it was in fact bush-league. And then I asked him about this DeLeo character.

"I'd go to him myself," Dr. Potler replied without hesitation. "I'd send my own family to him!" And so, partly out of laziness, partly because I wanted to miss as little work as possible, and finally because Dr. Potler had put my concerns to rest, I decided to keep my treatments local. I would see what Dr. DeLeo and Berkshire Hematology & Oncology had to offer, I told everyone… and then, if that generated any concerns, I would of course seek an additional opinion elsewhere.

* * * * * * * *

At the age of fifty-four, Dr. Michael DeLeo was balding handsomely, his hairline in full retreat along a pattern that conjured imagery of Jack Nicholson or Sean Connery. I felt completely comfortable with him right away. Upon greeting me for the first time, he instantly cracked a genuinely friendly smile and offered a firm, golf addict's handshake. If his bloodlines were predominantly Italian, as his surname implied, then his minerally-blue eyes suggested a rare strain from Sicily, or, more likely, from Italy's mountainous north. Might the DeLeo clan have originated in the sub-alpine Emilia-Romagna region, the birthplace of the likely Hodgkin Lymphoma discoverer Marcello Malpighi nearly four centuries ago? Dr. DeLeo wasn't all that familiar with the exact origins of his ancestors, nor, actually, did he seem particularly interested in the possibility of such a coincidental connection. This was business.

Like the vast majority of new medical school graduates, the young Dr. DeLeo had entertained no overwhelming desire to eventually become, of all things, an oncologist. However, when the time to choose a specific professional path approached, Dr. DeLeo objectively weighed such variables as income and lifestyle associated with his set of career options. Anesthesiology had seemed like the perfect fit... except that Dr. DeLeo absolutely loathed the idea of becoming an anesthesiologist. The day-to-day practice of oncology, however, presented a set of unique problems and their potential solutions that agreed with his particular thought processes, just as a medical school graduate with precise hands and a predilection for fixing things might have gravitated toward surgery.

As we sat together in the tiny examination room for our first appointment, Dr. DeLeo exuded competence as well as confidence, a grasp of his craft as sure-handed as his grip on his putter. And yet I immediately detected something of an unbreachable psychological moat around him, a self-protective emotional distance that he maintained from his patients. Oncology must be a heartbreaking business, I assumed. Despite the best efforts of the best doctors, patients regularly died. And even with a likely curable Hodgkin Lymphoma patient such as me, getting too close or familiar might make a perfunctory course of treatment feel a little bit like trying to sink a routine putt with money on the line and lots of people watching.

"No," Dr. DeLeo would protest months later as we conversed about the topic. "All branches of medicine have their heartbreaks." Obstetrics, for instance, might seem like a purely joyful specialty, welcoming fresh little babies into the world on a daily basis. But the downside, Dr. DeLeo pointed out, the loss of a newborn, could be many times more devastating than the inevitable passing of a terminally ill patient for whom one had done everything humanly and scientifically possible.

Scientifically possible... Perhaps that phrase was the water in the moat, the mantra that kept oncologists like Dr. DeLeo and his BHO colleagues from quitting or going insane. From observing them in their work as best I could, I tried to imagine what it must be like to be presented with a new cancer patient—

You go by the book, the accumulated case histories of countless other patients. You treat him like a unique individual, of course, but you also see him as a "case" of this carcinoma or that. You cleave faithfully unto the existing, established science; you offer the best treatment possible, and you explain its underlying justification as best you can, given the patient's ability and willingness to comprehend. You do everything just as the science says you should, and in rare circumstances you even add a new and significant case study to the existing body of experience, authoring a new page in the medical canon upon which your fellow doctors might base future decisions. And when, despite your best efforts, one of your patients dies, you assure yourself that you had done everything *scientifically possible*, soothing your bloodied psyche enough for you to take your hard-won lessons back to the war on cancer, back to the battlefield where next year's victories in similar cases become, through experiences such as yours, incrementally more achievable.

The battlefront in this war on cancer was being favorably advanced at the Berkshire Hematology & Oncology office in Pittsfield, or so it appeared to my fresh eyes immediately upon arriving for my first scheduled appointment. The prevailing mood felt cheerful and optimistic rather than dismal and depressing. The nursing and support staffs were smiling and friendly, and even the décor was colorful and comforting. Here in a newish, 9,500-square-foot brick building set among tall evergreens around the corner from Guido's, Dr. DeLeo and his fellow doctors established and pursued goals for their patients that would have been impossible just a few decades ago— a few more comfortable months in this world, or perhaps long-term "management," or, in my case and in an ever-increasing number of others, complete remission and a cure.

* * * * * * * *

"Before we can treat you, we need to stage you," Dr. DeLeo declared during that first appointment. As cancer had first appeared to be treatable in the 1950's, "staging," or determining the extent of the illness, became a vitally important tool in deciding upon the optimal course of treatment. For Hodgkin Lymphoma, what is known as the "Ann Arbor" system is used:

Stage I
The cancer is located in a single region, usually one lymph node and the surrounding area. Stage I often will not have outward symptoms.

Stage II
The cancer is located in two separate regions, an affected lymph node or organ within the lymphatic system and a second affected area, but both affected areas are on the same side of the diaphragm.

Stage III
The cancer has spread to the other side of the diaphragm, including one organ or area near the lymph nodes or the spleen.

Stage IV
The cancer has spread to the liver, the bone marrow, or the lungs.

In addition, one's stage may be further specified by the letter "A" indicating no obvious physical symptoms, or "B" indicating the presence of symptoms such as significant weight loss, night sweats, or chronic fatigue. Fortunately for HL patients, even Stage IVB has a high survival rate.

Meanwhile, perhaps to counterbalance my secret fears with gallows humor, my acid-tongued inner cynic conjured a parallel cancer staging system—

Stage I— *Confirm the status of your health insurance.*

Stage II— *Confirm the status of your LIFE insurance.*

Stage III— *Notarize your will.*

Stage IV— *Don't buy any green bananas.*

In the old days, I would be undergoing a surgical procedure— the staging laparotomy— to accurately assess my status. However, in the spring of 2008 all that was required of me was a bone marrow biopsy and a PET-scan.

The bone marrow biopsy was an extremely important key to my curative process. If my cancer had not yet crossed the threshold into my bones, my treatments would be relatively straightforward. On the other hand, the spread of cancer into my skeleton would raise the battle against it to a considerably higher level. Only by directly examining a sample of my bone tissue could Dr. DeLeo know where I stood. The procedure sounded rather easy; after what Dr. Namon had recently put me through, how hard could anything else be? How quickly I learned…

For my bone marrow biopsy, a phalanx of BHO nursing personnel (including a new young graduate on the morning of her first day) accompanied me into the usual small examination room. But rather than the usual exam table, this one had a bed— red flag number one. Then they told me to loosen my pants and lie face down— another red flag and-a-half. And then one of the senior nurses brought her lips close to my right ear— "*It's okay to scream if you need to,*" she reassuringly whispered, as if to put me more at ease. Was I about to be ravaged like a pink-cheeked cabin boy on the high seas?

Finally, Dr. DeLeo dashed into the room… hastily, as if about to perform a task that he found distasteful. He immediately injected a spot of skin on my lower back with Novocain, and then, without waiting quite long enough for the anesthetic to take full effect, he traced a slit across the relevant area with what felt to me like a rusty box-cutter. The sudden silence in the room as he brought the next tool into view was broken when the new girl involuntarily gasped. I refused to look, but I surmised that the implement in question probably resembled an apple corer or some such thing. For the next few minutes Dr. DeLeo repeatedly plunged whatever this was deep into the very marrow of my pelvis, well beyond the reach of the Novocain, with what felt like his full body weight.

And then, as abruptly as he had begun, he was done. "Didn't that *hurt?*" he asked.

"I wouldn't know," I calmly and defiantly replied as I zipped my jeans. "I was rowing."

Indeed, I had been able to completely tune out the physical reality of what might well have resembled a miniature ax-murder by once again fantasizing myself atop a Concept2 ergometer. In this instance, my powerful imagination had teleported me into a grueling 2,000-meter erg race, desperately straining for oxygen while stroking through the flames of anaerobic hell in the last few meters before the finish. And Dr. DeLeo thought that this *bone marrow biopsy* should have hurt? *F-U-C-K* him! This golfer had no idea what *real* pain was, I privately chortled…

…He had no way of knowing that rowers could eat his bone marrow biopsy for breakfast.

Next came the PET ("Positron Emission Tomography") scan, a far less invasive and academically more fascinating test than the gruesome bone-coring I had just managed to endure.

Positrons, the anti-matter of electrons, are sub-atomic particles that were never even observed until 1932, four years after their existence had been initially theorized by a British physicist. Certain radioactive atoms decay by emitting positrons and thereby, to a specific type of detection device, pinpoint their exact positions even from deep within the human body. Cancer cells require an inordinate amount of sugar to facilitate their rapid reproduction. By using sugar molecules as Trojan-horse-like vessels for this type of radioactivity, medical science can identify in three-dimensional imagery the areas of high sugar uptake within the body— "hot spots" that are most likely cancerous.

My PET-scan procedure began with a strict fast the night before, as my blood would need to be completely void of sugar for the exam. A boisterously energetic and instantly lovable giant of a medical technician named Scott led me from the BHO waiting room outside to the multi-million-dollar trailer in the parking lot. There Scott gave me a small injection of "FDG"— Fluorodeoxyglucose, or, more succinctly, radioactive sugar. Then I was sent back to the BHO waiting room, where I was required to relax, perhaps meditate, but not even allowed to read magazines as we waited for the FDG to be absorbed. Any physical activity, Scott explained, might skew the readings. Forty-five minutes later I was back in Scott's trailer, lying on a sliding gurney in a set-up very much like that of a CT-scan as highly sophisticated positron receptors mapped in microscopic detail my cancerous tissue.

The results from these two tests were as encouraging as could be expected— no evidence of cancer in my bone marrow or anywhere else other than my neck and chest. "As I expected, you're Stage IIA," explained Dr. DeLeo. "Which means that I could cure you with chemotherapy alone, or radiation alone." But by using some of each rather than all of one or the other, he explained, he would minimize the long-term negative effects of my treatment. I found it reassuring to learn that HL has been so curable for so long that oncologists have been able to observe the effects of chemotherapy and radiation on survivors twenty or thirty years hence. Much of the present HL research, therefore, was devoted to plumbing the minimum treatment actually necessary to effect a total cure.

Now that I was staged, I would still need two more tests, the measurements of my heart and lung functioning. These would provide Dr. DeLeo a basis for later assessing the likely irreversible damage inflicted upon them by chemotherapy and radiation. After that the actual cancer treatments would commence. For the chemo portion of my treatment, Dr. DeLeo would attack my tumors not with a single anti-cancer agent, but rather with a combination of four different drugs, each with its own mechanism for destroying malignant cells and each with a different deleterious side effect on my body. In this manner, he would democratically distribute the collateral damage among my various organs while more effectively attacking the cancer. A single chemo drug, explained Dr. DeLeo, would soon lose its effectiveness as my cancer cells adapted to it, much like a major-league hitter solving a hard-throwing but nonetheless predictable pitcher.

Although he didn't look anything like a baseball player, Dr. DeLeo was assuming, in a way, the role of a starting pitcher, one member of a team's five-man starting rotation. Starters take the mound to begin sometimes thirty or more games per season. They are expected to last seven or eight innings each start, and thus tend to face each batter perhaps three or four times in a game. This is why such a pitcher needs to have mastered a variety of pitches— even if he could throw 100MPH fastballs on every pitch, his opposing hitters would soon get a bead on them and start jacking them over the fence by the fifth inning. Such a blazing fastball, therefore, is effective only when coyly alternated with pitches of contrasting speed and trajectory. With what repertoire of weapons was this pitcher named DeLeo proposing to mow down my cancer? Like most other Hodgkin patients, I would be receiving the time-tested, state-of-the-art ABVD regimen— four different chemo drugs equivalent, in a sense, to a pitcher's fastball, curveball, change-up, and slider.

"Oh..." Dr. DeLeo added at the end of my final pre-chemo appointment, with what might have been taken for a twinkle of cockiness in his cerulean eyes. "If you want to go to Boston for a second opinion, just let us know... we'll even set it up for you. We won't be offended." Nowadays, Hodgkin Lymphoma was treated pretty much the same way everywhere, he declared, and the cancer bigwigs at Dana-Farber would surely suggest the very same course of treatment that he was offering me.

But if I was ready to start my treatments at BHO, Dr. DeLeo continued, he would need to write me two prescriptions to coincide with the start of my chemotherapy— a three-pill anti-nausea regimen (Emend) and a second vial of pills to combat the gout that would otherwise be caused by the release of uric acid from my suddenly dying cancer cells. Dr. DeLeo's certainty that my body would soon be flush with such carnage reminded me right then of the brilliant South Vietnamese army officer described by General Norman Schwarzkopf in his memoirs. Notwithstanding the unfortunate final outcome of the overall conflict, this officer of the Army of the Republic of Vietnam (ARVN) was, by General Schwarzkopf's knowledgeable reckoning, a born military genius.

As Schwarzkopf sat with him in the sand-bagged safety of headquarters, the diminutive, chain-smoking *ARVN* officer explained in precise detail to his fighting men how his proposed ambush would trap the enemy against a nearby river, right down to the hours and minutes when such-and-such would happen. *"The enemy will be so surprised that they'll throw down their weapons and run*," he confidently predicted. "*Make sure you gather them.*" Schwarzkopf was somewhat taken aback— how could a responsible army officer be so sure of such things? Warfare is at best a murky and uncertain business. But then, to Schwarzkopf's amazement and delight, the ARVN troops returned a short while later, not only victorious but also carrying armfuls of abandoned enemy rifles.

I found myself impressed anew by Dr. DeLeo's sure-handed mien right then. If I had detected a whiff or two of cockiness amidst his confident airs, I'm sure that he had likewise caught a powerful gust of it behind my superficial bravado. We were going to make a great team.

One cannot actively choose one's beliefs; rather, they arise naturally in one's consciousness, like plants from seeds. And just as flowering trees don't bloom until their roots are firmly established, personal faith in a particular tenet requires a similarly sound basis of experiential evidence. Those ARVN troops had long known in their bones that they could thoroughly trust their commanding officer. Likewise, I had come to understand with near certainty that I would be safe under Dr. DeLeo's knowledgeable care. All I would have to do was take his bitter medicine, and surely it would make me all better.

No, I wouldn't be bothering with any trips to Boston, at least not at this point in the battle… I would be sending Dr. Michael DeLeo to the mound as my Ace in the most important game of my life.

* * * * * * * *

After arranging for my heart and lung tests, Dr. DeLeo scheduled the first of my eight chemotherapy sessions for Friday, May 30… exactly nine weeks after I first found the telltale lump, and just five days after what would be the single most important day of my entire life— that of my walk down the wedding aisle beside Mrs. Andrea Lee Whitcomb-May in the presence of God, family, friends, and the spirits of a dozen or so gurus at the Assisi Institute in Rochester, New York.

How To Throw A Wedding In 20 Days

Andrea had proposed to me, but it was I who suggested moving our wedding way up, a few days ahead of my chemotherapy treatments. On Monday, May 5, we agreed that we would get married on May 25, the Sunday of Memorial Day Weekend. Here's how we pulled it off.

Before firming up any plans, Andrea insisted that she first confer with Lynn K., her dear friend and likely maid-of-honor, as May 25 was also her birthday. No problem there. Now, successful couples tend to see eye-to-eye on certain fundamental issues such as finances, and Andrea and I wholeheartedly concurred that most people spend ridiculous amounts of money on their wedding arrangements. (Easy for us to say, of course, with the little money we actually had at our disposal.) With a little creativity, we figured, we could circumvent the costliest aspects of a wedding without detracting at all from the day's requisite majesty and pomp. Paradoxically, time was on our side, in a sense, for there simply weren't enough hours and days in which to spend the usual five figures on a caterer, a DJ, tuxedoes and dresses, a banquet hall, a florist, and a limo… all of which are typically booked much farther in advance than this. By disposing of all of these items— "sacred cows" at most weddings— we started with a blank slate and only concerned ourselves with what was actually possible.

The first order of business was the bling. Remember that advertisement a few years ago that suggested "three month's salary" as a helpful formula for choosing the correct engagement rock? Well, to be honest, that's about what I spent on my new Hyundai. One can hardly begrudge the diamond industry such chutzpah, but we declined to incorporate their helpful guideline into our selection process. Instead, we saved ourselves nine or ten grand when Andrea pulled from her jewelry box an antique ring that had belonged to her great-aunt. A friend of hers had it fitted to her slender finger as a wedding gift. And the wedding bands? Nothing wrong with the hundred-dollar versions they sell at Target, at least as viewed from a few feet away. We could replace them down the road should we suddenly find ourselves flush, we told ourselves.

While we were at Target we surrendered to the impulse to officially register our wedding intentions. We raced through the store with the little price-zapper gun they had handed us, excitedly pointing and clicking at every kitchen gadget and set of sheets that struck our fancy. Our friends and relatives would then be able to log onto Target's website and view the items on our wish list, and purchase them on-line. They could even have them shipped directly to us, if they wanted.

We had our rings, and next we needed to find an altar at which to exchange them. Back when we had been planning an autumn wedding, we had originally considered scoping out larger, less obvious venues such as local college theaters and grange halls. But now, with time much shorter, we turned to the Assisi Institute of Rochester, New York, where Andrea was studying *Kriya* yoga. Assisi's Director, Reverend Craig Bullock, was a respected psychotherapist as well as a licensed clergyman, and he generously consented to host and perform the ceremony. The Assisi Institute occupied a suite of rooms in an unremarkable-looking office building. However, its large meeting room was simultaneously dark and colorful, soothingly silent and yet bursting with sacred imagery. Andrea was confident that her fellow *Kriya-bons* would further beautify this powerfully serene space with plenty of flowers and candles.

That I would personally cater the reception was already a given. The ingredients were available to me at wholesale prices, and I was an experienced enough kitchen hand to make the food come out pretty much as I wished. Because we would be holding a mid-to-late afternoon reception, a hot, sit-down meal was not expected. We would simply offer a buffet of exotic salads and finger food, including plenty of shrimp. The menu was simple enough that we probably would have been able to serve it in the lobby of Assisi's building, if necessary. But Andrea's cousin Laurie, who lived nearby, volunteered her immaculately maintained home and backyard garden for our reception. Now all we had to do was figure out what to wear.

Guys are easy. I took a pre-existing, medium-gray wool suit of mine to a talented tailor in Pittsfield and had it disassembled and re-fit to my current form for $70, a tenth of what it had originally cost. I added a contrasting, dove-grey vest, a sartorial touch that instantly made me appear much more groom-like. By pairing a white cotton "piqué" bowtie ($15) with a similarly simple white shirt, my salmon-pink pocket square was my only dash of bright color, the better to allow the bridal party's various aquamarine ensembles to radiate without interference.

My bride wore a dress— not a gown, but fancy enough— that she had ordered on-line. Andrea forwarded photos of it to her bridal party, enabling them to match the color and thereby make a cohesive and more interesting visual impression than if they had been wearing identical dresses. We were even spared the usual expense of matching shoes, as the ceremony, per Assisi's rules, would be barefoot for all.

Thanks to iTunes, wedding music was ridiculously easy for us to assemble... no DJ necessary. And unless one needs a massive wall of decibels to drive the action on a dance floor, a fifty-dollar pair of mini-speakers can plug right into a lap-top and blare one's chosen playlist during and after the ceremony... all for a dollar a pop, or for free if one already owns them on CD. Andrea and I had fun assembling various discs for the ceremony and the reception, and I couldn't resist including for old times' sake a series of classic "car crash" songs— "Dead Man's Curve," "Last Kiss," "Leader of the Pack," and such.

We diligently rushed through the rest of our checklist. I made a trip to Family & Probate Court in Pittsfield to get an official copy of my divorce decree ($20) and then to Pittsfield's City Hall for my stamped birth certificate (another $10.) Andrea did the same on her end, and then we convinced the clerk in her Penfield, New York town hall to process our marriage license without the necessary appointment to do so.

Amazingly, everything was falling into place even while Andrea was working a tightly packed performing schedule in Rochester and I was juggling medical appointments and full work-weeks in the Berkshires. My son Remi and my daughter Rhys (ages 20 and 18, respectively) would be joining us for the ceremony, as would my long-time close friend Andy from Boston, who had been my best man the last time I exchanged rings. My brother Andrew and his family and my sister Sarah and hers would all arrive in Rochester on Friday night with our mother. Susannah, my other sister, wouldn't be able to break free from her demanding schedule down in Florida, but she invited us down for Christmas.

I was needed at work all day on Saturday the twenty-fourth at Guido's— we were short-staffed, and there was no way around it. I would leave Pittsfield at 7:00PM that evening with a carload of ingredients and head to Rochester, pick the kids up at the airport around midnight, and then get up at 6:00AM to prepare all of the food. But shortly after I arrived at work on Saturday, Remi phoned to tell me that he wouldn't be allowed past the airport's boarding gate because he had lost his only photo ID. "But I'm definitely gonna get there," he vowed. "I'm NOT gonna miss this!" A short while later he called back to tell me that three of his friends had agreed to make the sixteen-hour road trip with him in a borrowed car. (A *borrowed car...* ah, the irony and the echoes!) Before I hung up, I inquired whether his pals might be restaurant workers, as I would probably need their help setting up the reception food.

The early Sunday morning hours steadily melted away as I methodically put together an afternoon garden party feast for sixty people. Rhys, as always, was a trooper in the kitchen, collaborating smoothly with me despite our mutual sleep deprivation as we finished and sealed up one dish after another. Remi and his friends met me at a nearby coffee shop around 10:00AM after I guided them by phone along the last few miles of highway. They made it in time! With the food all prepared and securely packed on ice, we took turns showering and then got dressed for the ceremony... without Andrea, of course, who was readying herself with her bridesmaids. She had insisted that I not see her that day until she approached the Assisi altar on her father's arm.

* * * * * * * *

While I was still in Massachusetts, Andrea had calmly gone about her busy bridal weekend. She had previously booked the day before the wedding as a workday, appearing in character as "Greta Garbage," her environmentally-educating alter ego. Purely by fortunate coincidence, her appearance that morning included some time with her Assisi "family" of fellow *Kriya-bons* as she joined them for a fundraising hike in Rochester. As she walked, Andrea wore a sign on her back that read, "Almost Married." At the hike's conclusion, Andrea saw nothing unusual about inviting everyone within earshot— friend and stranger alike— to our wedding. And then she ran off to see her grandmother, who had just been admitted to the emergency room... all while I was busy slicing fish and selling wine at Guido's, three hundred miles away.

Late that afternoon, Andrea joined my family for a relaxed and fun wedding rehearsal at the Assisi Institute, *sans* groom. My sister-in-law Yvonne (brother Andrew's wife) stood in my place.

"So... does this mean they're married?" quipped my brother after the practice vows.

"Only in Massachusetts!" replied Craig.

After the practice wedding came a rehearsal dinner hosted by Andrea's new mother-in-law at Beale Street Restaurant in nearby Webster. My absence probably afforded my mother and the rest of my family that much better an opportunity to get to know Andrea, I told myself.

As Sunday dawned, the bright, calm Rochester sky foretokened one of the most beautiful spring days of the year in this normally overcast and windy region of the United States. After a refreshing morning in meditation, Andrea casually shopped Rochester's public market for fresh, locally grown roses, gifts that she would present to a few of her closest friends and family members as part of our wedding ceremony. My mother and Andrea's stepmother would find this especially touching. Andrea enjoyed a free breakfast, courtesy of a public market food stand operator after he learned of her imminent nuptials. While waiting in line for her food, Andrea spotted a woman wearing the telltale chemo head scarf and initiated a conversation with her about my upcoming treatments. The woman wished us good health and congratulated us on our new life together.

Much to her surprise, Andrea was actually able to relax in the last hours before the ceremony, perhaps because there was actually very little remaining for her to do… or maybe it was because she was surrounded by close and joyful friends who wanted to contribute in any way possible to making her wedding day a beautiful occasion. Everyone was pitching in— Andrea's father had even stepped forward at the last minute to help assemble gorgeous wedding shawls to be worn by the bridal party. Of course Andrea's stepmother had done most of the actual sewing, but it was sweet that her father contributed as much as he did to the effort.

I had been so preoccupied with making so much happen— getting my kids (and myself) to Rochester, sourcing and preparing the food— that it didn't actually strike me as my wedding day until I reached the Assisi Institute itself. Having accomplished so much during the preceding weeks and hours, I was suddenly able to relax and drink in the beauty of the scene. The weather was impossibly splendid for Rochester, and everyone was buzzing with excitement and joy… and I was about to marry the love of my life.

* * * * * * * *

A hush came over the gathered guests as Andrea entered the room beside her father accompanied by "Our Prayer," a surprisingly spiritual *a capella* chant by, of all bands, the Beach Boys. It was an especially fitting song for the occasion, actually— Brian Wilson, the band's gifted but troubled composer, had taken thirty-eight years to complete his masterpiece "SMiLE" album on which this cut is featured, only slightly longer than Andrea and I had taken to reunite.

As Andrea came into my view a few feet from the altar, her eyes were practically ablaze, so bursting with love that it seemed as though I might be knocked over by the intensity of her gaze. Craig's rite of marriage was a masterful blend of Judeo-Christian sentiments, wisdom from the gurus, and practical advice from a professional psychologist. "As you wish," Craig claimed, was the most important sentiment exchanged between husband and wife… the words that signified melting into each other's hearts.

The emotional climax of the ceremony came when we exchanged the vows that we had written ourselves—

ANDREA:

My beloved & stunning Danny, you dwell at the core of my being with God,
as God's reflection of pure Love.
To you I surrender my mortal love blessed by Love itself.
Each moment is joy.
I shall recognize the pain as fully as the pleasure
knowing it is God living wholly through each experience of our union,
merging each breath with yours.
The Divine in me blissfully marries the Divine in you.

DANNY:

I've prayed for this day since I was a young teenager.

Today I pray for sufficient wisdom to understand the will of the Divine… for today, just like so many years ago, God seems to shine His light upon me through Andrea's eyes. To love Andrea, therefore, is to bask in the warmth and illumination of heavenly rays.

And yet part of me cannot help but wistfully consider the days, the years, the decades that Andrea and I might have blissfully shared, time irretrievably lost to history. What could possibly have been God's purpose in forestalling our togetherness for so long?

But my prayers for wisdom are answered as I am mindful that every day of all those years— every triumph, every tear— were each necessary steps along the paths that finally re-unite us here today. As I now stand here and consider everything in my past and present life—and do I mean EVERYTHING—I know that I am the most fortunate man on Earth.

And so on this blessed day, my dearest Andrea, I gratefully, humbly, and proudly become your loving husband, now and for the future that God has reserved for us.

We had a makeshift receiving line at Assisi, and several of Andrea's last-minute invitees came through the line. We posed for a few pictures before driving over to the reception. Once there, the Georgia kids and I seized control of the kitchen and began assembling the platters. Here's what we served—

Reception Menu

Scandinavian Potato Salad
Red potatoes with mayonnaise, sour cream, mustard, chopped fresh dill, and red onion.

Shrimp Cocktail with Classic Cocktail Sauce and Homemade Pesto
The trick to great shrimp cocktail is to make it the same day you eat it, and quickly— use a huge pot of boiling water, and then chill them ice-cold ASAP.

Deluxe Tuna Salad
What makes it "deluxe" is the addition of little bursts of flavor— capers, pickle relish, lemon oil, and finely chopped roasted peppers. Also, don't scrimp on the tuna; pay a little more for much higher quality.

Curried Chicken Salad
There are a few useful tricks for this dish-- using good, properly cooked chicken, soaking the currants to soften them, grating fresh ginger, and lightly heating the curry powder in oil before adding it.

Pasta Vegetable Salad
Combine good pasta with fresh veggies and high-quality olive oil, and you don't need much else. One little touch of mine in salads like this is reduced balsamic vinegar.

Assorted Cheeses & Salami
We had other fabulous stuff on these platters, like white anchovies and assorted olives. This dish is all about the shopping.

Fresh Guacamole & Tortilla Chips
This isn't a football game— buy the best chips, and make real guacamole with perfectly ripe avocadoes, freshly chopped cilantro, and fresh-squeezed lime juice.

Rebecca's Breads
Rebecca is the pre-eminent guerrilla baker in the Berkshires. You have to know her to get her outrageously delicious home-made bread, but there's probably a Rebecca in every community, if you can find her.

We toasted the day with Santome extra dry Prosecco, an inexpensive and delicious Italian sparkling wine that is perfect for such occasions. Everyone knew that I was in the wine business, but no one really came to the wedding reception expecting a wine tasting. Our guests also drank San Pelligrino sparkling water, Izze sodas (blueberry and tangerine) Guinness stout, and Yuengling lager.

After the reception, Andrea and I kept an important promise by visiting her ninety-three-year-old grandmother in the hospital while still in our wedding clothes. Though bedridden, she had actually been present at our wedding, in a way— cousin Laurie had used Grandma's applesauce spice cake recipe for our wedding cake.

The old woman's eyes sparkled almost as brightly as Andrea's when we entered her hospital room as husband and wife, granddaughter and new grandson. She wouldn't be around for much longer, we knew, and I was very pleased to have had the honor of getting to know her and her feisty sense of humor.

"Do you have any… you know, *advice* for our wedding night?" I couldn't resist asking her.

"I don't think you two need any!" she laughed.

And then we went to the lake. When my family first moved to the Rochester area in 1964, Lake Ontario's vastness amazed us young children. Unlike the tiny lakes in and around our native Pittsfield, Lake Ontario was too big to see across, and thus, to a child's mind, perhaps infinite. Whenever one of us makes a rare visit to Rochester, we almost always make a point of going down to gaze at the lake, a brief pilgrimage to reacquaint ourselves with its enormity. Andrea and I had no trouble convincing Andrew and Sarah and their families to join us at Seabreeze, a micro-community of burger joints along Ontario's sands seemingly unaltered by the passage of the previous half-century.

We ordered the usual, deliciously grease-fried fare as we familiarized the young cousins with the local culinary terminology— a "ground round" was a hamburger; and hot dogs came in two types, "white hot" for a brat-like, white version, and "red hot" for the more familiar-looking type. After eating, we made our way over to the giant lake's edge, the northern border of the United States. The late-May sun would soon set into Ontario's western waters, which had fallen dead calm— just as they had when Andrea and I took our fateful stroll on the very same beach the previous January.

Back in Penfield, Andrea and I surrendered her house to Rhys and Remi and the other Georgia kids while we took a room in a nice hotel right down the road as the hour grew late. The long day, the full week, the busy preceding month… it had all been quite exhausting for both of us. Pulling off a wedding such as ours in so little time would have been an amazing accomplishment even without our crammed work schedules, numerous medical appointments, and so many miles between us for most of time.

But we seemed to have been pulled along through the process by mysterious forces, and thus it was impossible not to interpret the unbelievable beauty of everything that day— the moving ceremony, the delightful reception, the perfect weather, and the joy so clearly evident on every face— as heavenly approval of our union. Accordingly, we both felt sufficiently energized even as the clock struck midnight to defer sleep in the tradition of newlyweds immemorial, and our hotel tab turned out to be money well spent. It seemed like only a few short hours later when, still lovingly entwined, we groggily answered an alarm clock for the very first time as Mr. and Mrs. May.

My chemotherapy was scheduled to begin exactly four mornings later.

"I have heard there are troubles of more than one kind.
Some come from ahead and some come from behind. But
I've bought a big bat. I'm all ready you see. Now my
troubles are going to have troubles with me!"

(Dr. Seuss)

THE CHEMO SALON

By God, it had finally, really happened... Andrea and I had just gotten married, less than five months after re-meeting in person, and with nearly five full U.S. Presidencies between our last teenage date and the present. Upon arising that Monday morning as newly wedded husband and wife, our new status had not yet completely sunk in to either of us; rather, it still felt like young, adolescent love, the exact physical and emotional rush that I had experienced while trailing young Andrea through Wayne Central's halls so long ago. How long could such euphoria possibly last?

As Andrea approached me at the Assisi altar the day before, the otherworldly light in her eyes that had radiated upon me throughout our ceremony was as powerful a beam as I have ever felt— as dazzling as that day's brilliant sun, as piercing as x-rays. She *had* me, I'm sure she must have realized; she owned me, she possessed me completely. She knew that I could never, ever lie to her, cheat on her, or intentionally do anything to hurt her. But I found it impossible not to therefore wonder— how might it be that she had finally come to love me just as much? Was it only because she had suddenly realized how deeply I had loved her for so long? Because at last I had been able to show her the secure place that I had kept for her in my heart for all of these years?

In cases like this (though I know of no exact equivalent) it is probably best not to over-dissect the mysteries of human feelings and just simply be thankful for one's improbable, unequaled fortune. The New Testament parable of the workers in the vineyard (Matthew 20:1-15) seemed analogous— laborers who had reported for work in the harvest's eleventh hour were compensated with a full day's pay, much to the grumbling of those who had toiled since sunrise. But in the eyes of the landlord, all who had come to him that day merited equal reward. Likewise, given that Andrea had finally fallen as completely in love with me as I had with her so many years before, of what importance, really, was the timing of her epiphany relative to mine? Our divinely-intended togetherness had been awaiting the proper alignment of the necessary components, apparently. Now, at last, we were awash in the pure essence of heavenly love itself, realized in the here and now. Little else mattered.

Besides, to be fair I must confess to feeling doubly fortunate, for I was simultaneously in love with not one but two Andreas— the jewel-eyed, shy but kind-hearted fourteen year-old whom I had "discovered" just ahead of the hungry pack; and the beautiful, grown-up woman now beside me. At the age of forty-eight, Andrea still looked well shy of her fourth decade. World-wise and confident, she was maybe a little love-scarred and encumbered by her past relationships, but even larger of heart and happier of soul than ever. She had me securely in her palm, she knew, but I now held *both* of her in mine.

We spent a quiet Monday together in Rochester tying up loose ends from the magical day before. Rhys got to meet her new great-grandmother in the hospital on the way to the airport, and it was touching to watch the old woman's alert eyes repeatedly dart between my daughter and me, assaying the genetic connection so obvious in our bone structure and coloring. We packed up party platters and empty bottles at cousin Laurie's house, and then puttered about Andrea's Penfield home as our wedding day palpably slipped further into memory by the hour. I left for the Berkshires very early the next morning to resume my usual work schedule, and Andrea followed on her own a few hours later.

In the aftermath of our rather impromptu wedding, there would be no honeymoon in the traditional sense of the term, nothing even close... no luxury cruise, no trip to Niagara Falls or Hawaii. Having just pulled off an entire wedding for less money than most couples drop on airfare for such getaways, we weren't about to spend funds that were not yet ours just to make love in an unfamiliar zip code for a week or two. Besides, we had a pressing matter awaiting my return to the Berkshires— eight sessions of combination chemotherapy, scheduled for every other Friday throughout the busy summer work season of 2008. This, for better or worse, for richer and poorer, in sickness and in health, would be our honeymoon... our Chemo Honeymoon.

* * * * * * * * *

I arrived at Berkshire Hematology & Oncology's Pittsfield office in the early hours of Friday, May 30 for my first chemotherapy treatment. Andrea was unable to join me for this initial appointment because of her remaining performance commitments in Rochester. This was probably a good thing, I assured her... I would go through it myself the first time, and then I would be able to talk her through it next time as if I were an experienced hand. The appointment began with what would eventually become an iron routine— giving a blood sample for lab analysis, having my weight, pulse, and blood pressure checked by a nurse, and then a hands-on physical examination by the Ace himself, Dr. DeLeo. But this first chemo appointment— this first inning of the game of my life— suddenly felt a lot more serious than baseball... more like war.

A little after 10:00 AM, about two hours after I had arrived that morning, Dr. DeLeo directed me down the hall to the infusion room, almost as if parachuting me into battle. After two months of intelligence-gathering— blood-work, x-rays, CT-scans, PET-scans, biopsies, and surgery— the actual fighting was finally about to commence. While I was busy engaging the enemy in close personal combat, Dr. DeLeo, like any other war general, would remain secure behind the sandbags and sentries, there to

60

assess second-hand the lessons of the battlefield for future reference should I return limp and lifeless on my shield.

In other words, I was on my own... except for Elaine, my assigned chemo nurse and thus my closest comrade in my personal war against cancer.

Nurse Elaine stood tall and sturdy, her obvious physical fortitude beautifully complemented and feminized by her big, warm eyes and happy smile. It was a mix that exuded compassion and caring. If she maintained a protective psychological wall someplace to shield her from oncology's occupational agony, it was invisible to me.

I would be under Elaine's care every other Friday morning through Labor Day, she explained as she gave me a quick tour of the long, window-lined room. This was the "chemo salon," as I would later describe it to curious friends and family, separated into two wings by a central mixing station where the actual medicines were measured and prepared beneath an exhaust hood. Each side of the room had a row of six comfortably upholstered reclining chairs for us patients, somewhat like an old-school beauty parlor.

This was unlike any other medical facility I had ever seen. Amenities such as DVD's, wireless Internet service, knit blankets, and high-quality, fresh-brewed coffee were ours for the asking. Beside each of the chemo chairs stood a wheeled scaffold for hanging IV bags, the contents of which dripped through an electronic monitor en route to one's bloodstream. The wheels, explained Elaine, would enable me to use the bathroom without disconnecting my catheter, a feature that I would very soon have reason to appreciate.

I noticed right away that the BHO doctors themselves tended to avoid the infusion room itself, like dogs thoroughly disciplined by Invisible Fence... unless there arose a declared medical emergency (a "code," in medical-ese) such as an acute adverse reaction to a chemo drug. Otherwise, Elaine and five or so other chemo nurses ran the show from their glass-lined nursing stations, one for each wing. Right after I claimed my seat and plugged in my computer and phone, Elaine got down to business, carefully explaining every step of my chemotherapy process.

Andrea and I had been contemplating this inevitable day for the previous two months. Now that it had finally come, I was here by myself, facing the unknown. Was I scared?

One often reads about a relative or acquaintance who has passed away after his or her "brave battle with cancer." In contrast to the courageous game face I had been presenting to my co-workers, in reality I harbored no intention of embellishing my obituary with any such heroic references. I would sucker-punch my malignancy whenever possible, kick it in the nuts, hit it after the whistle, shoot it in the back, and do anything else it took to defeat it. And yet, to be honest, I felt no particular anger or antipathy toward my cancer cells. They were *me*, after all... progeny of my flesh, my wayward sons. Like fallen angels, they had turned bad, and yet I still loved them as I suppose God must still love Lucifer. However, I needed to banish them from my body, or else they would eventually kill me.

Everyone from Neal W. to Dr. DeLeo had made beating my cancer sound very doable. But I understood that even if I went through all of this tried-and-true chemotherapy and radiation, there was still a one-in-twenty chance that within five years this Hodgkin Lymphoma, this disease that had taught the world that cancer was survivable, would steal from me my future with Andrea, rob me of what seemed like my life's reward for everything I've ever been and done.

Yes, when I thought of things like this I was terrified... frightened to my quivering bones in those rare, middle-of-the-night moments when I could summon the strength to abandon my self-protective bravado and sob aloud for a moment in Andrea's warm and loving embrace—"I don't *want* to die! I'M SCARED!"

But I had a duty, I felt, to stand firm as an example to my co-workers and customers, to show them my courageous side... to show them that cancer could be faced and beaten... to show them that an erg racing champion and former NCAA place-kicker with a black belt in karate had the balls to unflinchingly laugh in the face of what was once certain death... and that if I could stare it down, then maybe they could, too, when their turn came. The only remaining obstacle, really, wasn't my fear of death, nor that my future with Andrea might be stolen by cancer. Rather, it was my lifelong dread of medical procedures, especially those involving blood and needles.

Two weeks before my first scheduled chemo treatment, I had declined a surgically-implanted port through which I could have more easily received my injections… seemingly, to some at BHO, as a condemned prisoner might opt to be dispatched without a blindfold. My well-exercised veins protruded prominently, I had protested. Besides, I was physically active at work; I had no intention of suspending my rowing workouts; and I was a newlywed, after all, and planned on being naked in bed on a regular basis. Having some Frankenstein-ish plastic pipe semi-permanently implanted in my chest had sounded both inconvenient and a little gruesome. Gimme your needles straight into my pipes, I had more or less demanded, as if accepting an unspoken dare.

My life was now in Nurse Elaine's hands. After I explained to her why I was without the usual port, she carefully inspected my lower right arm for just the right type of vein ("not too *valve-y!*") and fitted it with an IV to accommodate the multiple injections I was going to receive over the next few hours. She gave me a second anti-nausea medication through the IV, and then a steroid to enable it in preparation for administering into my bloodstream the four different anti-cancer drugs.

* * * * * * * * *

Chemotherapy had come a long way in just a few decades. In the wake of the 1943 explosion of the *SS John Harvey* in Italy and its unexpectedly promising implications, U.S. Army researchers as well as others (most notably at Yale) began clinically testing the anti-cancer effectiveness of nitrogen mustard on patients. Other anti-cancer drugs, meanwhile, were likewise deployed as the effects of different toxins upon the mechanisms of cell reproduction became better understood.

The pediatric pathologist Dr. Sidney Farber (as in Dana-Farber) observed in 1947 that folic acid hastened the progression of certain leukemias, and correctly reasoned that "anti-folates" such as Aminopterin would have the opposite effect by blocking a chemical reaction necessary for DNA replication. Just a few years later, naturally-occuring compounds derived from certain tropical plants were also found to block cell division, though by a different mechanism.

Hodgkin Lymphoma proved to be particularly responsive to these chemical agents in early research, but it was not until the mid-1960's that chemistry alone could claim a cure. It was "combination chemotherapy," the simultaneous administration of different types of anti-cancer toxins, that by 1963 had finally established chemotherapy's efficacy against Hodgkin Lymphoma. The original combination of anti-HL chemotherapy drugs was known as "MOMP"— an acronym for the mustard derivative Mechlorethamine, Oncovin (the trade name for Vincristine, an alkaloid extracted from a flowering plant), the anti-folate Methotrexate (successor to Dr. Farber's Aminopterin), and Prednisone (a synthesized steroid that functions as an immunosuppressant.)

A year later the Methotrexate was replaced with Procarbazine, a synthesized alkylating agent that prevents the DNA coil separation necessary for cell reproduction. The improved regimen— re-christened MOPP— proved effective in achieving long survival rates… so long, in fact, that the medical community was able to assess the long-term effects of such poisonous agents on HL patients. MOPP's harsh toxicity inspired research into a milder, completely different regimen. In the mid-1970's, Italian scientists produced convincing data that led to the implementation of a new and different combination (ABVD), one at least as effective as MOPP but far less debilitating and toxic. The ABVD regimen— which I would be receiving— takes its name from "A" for Adriamycin; "B" for Bleomycin; "V" for Vinblastine; and "D" for Dacarbazine.

In essence, these drugs were all different forms of birth control that prevented cell reproduction, I concluded as I read as much as I could comprehend about them. Hell, condoms can break and pills can fail, but a sexually active couple that simultaneously employed four different contraceptives could expect with comfortable certainty to avoid the stork. Likewise, with the four different drugs they were about to give me, my cancer cells stood little chance of perpetuating their evil genealogy.

Adriamycin (a.k.a. the "red devil") is based on a compound originally isolated from fungi in the soil surrounding a thirteenth century Italian castle. It disrupts cell reproduction via "intercalation," a complex process by which chemical groups are interposed between DNA strands... almost like chaperones intrusively wedging themselves between back-seat teenage lovers at a drive-in and thereby forestalling their parenthood.

Deep crimson in color, Adriamycin navigates one's body so fast that the necessity of the wheels on the IV scaffold quickly became apparent. Soon after receiving my bagful, I hastened to the bathroom to discharge urine the exact coral-pink of the *Brut Rosé* champagne with which Andrea and I had toasted my favorable diagnosis just a few weeks before.

Bleomycin is another anti-cancer agent derived from dirt; to wit, bacteria discovered by Japanese researchers in fertile soil and rotting vegetation. Bleomycin prevents cell reproduction by breaking DNA strands... suggestive, to me anyway, of a painful sex-related injury that would immediately nix any likelihood of fertilization. A poison among poisons, Bleomycin is especially toxic to lung tissue and potentially fatal to those allergic to it. A tiny test dose, therefore, is carefully administered to first-time recipients.

Vinblastine is a chemical cousin of Vincristine, and likewise a vinca alkaloid compound extracted from the Madagascar periwinkle plant. This family of chemicals inhibit mitosis, the separation of cells into pairs of new, genetically identical offspring. As with an ovulating young belle securely holding a bible between her knees, the critical moment passes without the cancerous cells producing young ones.

Dacarbazine (trade name DTIC) is a synthesized alkylating agent that, like its predecessor Procarbazine, cross-links the two sides of the DNA double helix as it tries to separate at a crucial point in cell reproduction. Imagine an ardent couple inseparably super-glued together and thus unable to disrobe— different contraceptive mechanism, same result.

If these four drugs worked as Dr. DeLeo had promised, then indeed my system would soon be flush with dead and childless cancer cells.

* * * * * * * * *

At exactly 10:48AM, the first drops of my test dose of Bleomycin entered my bloodstream. The battle was on… my Chemo Honeymoon had officially begun, along with the battle of my life. I was finally inflicting some casualties, killing enemy cells, kicking cancer's ass. Hell, this chemo didn't seem all that bad, I thought. Two hours later it was surely the steroid enlivening me as I reported for work all full of pep, my right arm bandaged at the elbow where blood had been drawn, and at my wrist where I had been infused. One down, seven to go… I can do this, I thought, even as my suddenly ashen complexion elicited curious sidelong glances from my co-workers all afternoon.

On my way home from work I stopped at the Lenox Fitness Center, my training center for the past decade. I needed to make some sort of defiant statement. "Got a bucket?" I asked the stunned manager at the desk as he took notice of the bandages encircling my arm. Just as cancer was NOT going to rob me of my future with Andrea, its treatment was NOT going to stop me from rowing, dammit!

I set the ergometer for 5,000 meters and stroked away as the manager looked on in horror. If the nausea infamously associated with chemotherapy were to suddenly erupt, this might well be the time and place. Albert V. was fond of re-telling the story about one of his oncologists who ran into a former patient in an airport terminal, only to have the patient, purely out of Pavlovian conditioning from his chemotherapy, promptly vomit at his feet.

I never needed the bucket, as it turned out. The chemo-related nausea that was severe enough to have caused psychological damage among cancer patients just fifteen years before had been effectively neutralized by the Emend, and I successfully rowed all the way back to my virtual dock without incident.

Having made my point (if only to myself) I left the gym, brazenly making an illegal u-turn on 7 South. A Lenox policeman immediately pulled me over, and for the first time I played the "cancer card." He let me off with just a warning, nearly tearful after I explained the treatment I had endured that day. Things might have turned out quite differently had he realized that I was just coming from a rowing workout.

I was scheduled to work on Saturday as well, but after that I would have two consecutive days off in anticipation of the expected physical letdown. On Sunday morning Andrea and I would tend to what we felt was a pressing piece of cancer patient business. During my office appointment with Dr. DeLeo on Friday morning right before my first chemo treatment, he had mentioned something in passing as he exited the tiny exam room, a seemingly minor detail. "Oh, yeah, one more thing," he said as he paused and turned, Lieutenant Columbo-like...

"You're going to lose all of your hair."

Easy for him to say, the bald-headed son-of-a-bitch... was he actually smirking to himself as he said that?

JOINING THE ORDER

Andrea returned from Rochester late Saturday afternoon, the day after my first chemo treatment. Popular wisdom has it that chemotherapy is murder upon one's body and spirit, more devastating in some respects than the cancer itself. Nine years ago my ill father's theretofore iron resolve was nearly broken by chemotherapy's horrors en route to his grave, and a couple of years later his sister's husband had willingly chosen death over further infusions. But anti-nausea drugs and other mitigating medications had improved many-fold in recent years, and I felt strong enough to report for work on my first "morning after," well enough to select wine and fish for my customers that Saturday. But Dr. DeLeo had assured me that my series of eight scheduled treatments would exact an increasingly heavy toll on my physical strength and endurance as the summer progressed. In accordance with his recommendations, I would have the next two days off for my necessary rest.

Sunday, June first was my sister Sarah's fifty-second birthday. Andrea and I looked forward to spending a fun afternoon at her Saratoga home celebrating the occasion. On the way to her house from Great Barrington we ran two errands. First, I needed to make a quick stop at the chemo salon for a shot of Neulasta, a recently developed "miracle drug" for cancer patients that would boost my white blood cell count and thereby counteract one of the chemotherapy's more problematic side effects. This was necessary to protect me from infections to which I was suddenly more susceptible.

Medical miracles, however, can be exorbitantly expensive— out-of-pocket, one shot of Neulasta would have cost me $1600, much more than the street value of any sort of recreational drug presently in vogue.

According to the doctor who would oversee my radiation treatments, more money is spent on Neulasta alone for cancer patients in the United States than on the sum total exchanged for his branch of medicine.

After my quick and precious injection, Andrea and I then crossed the state border into Spencertown, New York, a tiny village within the Columbia County Town of Austerlitz. There, at the home of a lifelong family friend, we addressed errand number two—

Shaving my head.

* * * * * * * * *

June B. has resided in Spencertown since the waning months of the Johnson Administration. A fellow Pittsfield native, June had become friendly with both of my parents during college in the mid-1950's, and thus she has literally known me since the day I was born. We have always gotten on well, and she has often been like a second mother to me. June herself survived a terrifying illness in 2005. Ovarian cancer is often asymptomatic until death is nigh, and therefore has a relatively low survival rate. June was extremely lucky to have caught hers just in time. The first round of chemotherapy treatments didn't make her bald, but her ovarian cancer cells reappeared two years later in her lungs, and by December of 2007 she was completely hairless from the Taxol in her new chemo regimen. By the time I got sick in 2008, June's hair had grown back nicely.

Given June B's history, it made perfect sense to us that she would join Andrea for what seemed like the ritualistic removal of my hair.

I have never been bald, nor have I ever wished to be. For that matter, I have never even favored short hair over long. Now, some men look very good with pates of shiny skin. Some men, for a variety of reasons, choose to shave their (remaining) hair off. The combination chemotherapy to which I was being subjected was going to take that choice away from me. As I reviewed the primary side effects of my four chemo drugs, I realized what sort of beating my entire body, particularly my scalp, was in for—

Adriamycin— Cardio-toxicity (heart damage) and hair loss;

Bleomycin— Pulmonary toxicity (lung damage) and hair loss;

Vinblastine— Bone pain; constipation; depression; diarrhea; dizziness; general body discomfort; headache; jaw pain; loss of appetite; nausea; stomach pain; vomiting… and hair loss;

Dacarbazine— Immuno-suppression and sterility… alas, I would father no more offspring, but at least it wouldn't contribute to my hair loss.

Three out of four. Yep, whether I liked it or not, I was about to go completely bald.

* * * * * * * * *

Hair on a man has long been associated with power and virility, as much a symbol of manhood as the capability to father children that my Dacarbazine was about to nix. In the Old Testament Book of Judges, Samson is described as having God-given, superman-like strength, capable of tearing a lion limb-from-limb as well as slaying a thousand Philistines with only the jawbone of a donkey. The key to Samson's strength, it is written, rested in his full mane of hair; so long as it remained uncut, he would maintain his powerful physical advantage over the Philistines.

But if hair represents physical strength and prowess, then it follows that radically removing it signifies the opposite. Samson's wicked second wife, Delilah, was bribed by the Philistines to discover the source of her husband's strength. After a series of playful fibs, he reluctantly revealed his secret to her. She then had Samson's hair shorn while he slept, so thoroughly weakening him that he was finally taken prisoner by the Philistines, who promptly blinded him and then harnessed him to slave labor. To my vanity, chemo baldness was only marginally less harsh than the fate that befell poor Samson.

Chemotherapy drugs cause hair loss for the very same reason that they are so effective against cancer cells— as they simultaneously attack all cells in the body, they are particularly poisonous to fast-dividing cells, like carcinomas and hair follicles. Better to be bald and alive, one accepts, even if such sudden hairlessness is an immediate and highly visible manifestation of one's serious illness. Interestingly, perhaps, it places the cancer patient in the company of new United States Marines, prospective priests, and Parisian females accused of "horizontally collaborating" with their Nazi occupiers.

In many religions, monks are required to shave their heads upon joining their order as a sign of humility and submission, of leaving behind their worldly vanity as they seek a higher, more spiritual plane of existence. When I was a young teen in the early 1970's, my first exposure to eastern mysticism was the television show "Kung Fu." Every Saturday night beginning in the autumn of 1972, the wandering, half-Chinese priest Kwai Chang Caine karate-chopped his way through the American West of the late nineteenth century. Between the inevitable East-West dust-ups, we impressionable young viewers were fed TV-quality nuggets of Oriental wisdom from his bald Shaolin mentors—

"To suppress a truth is to give it force beyond endurance." — Master Kan

"Yet, it is eyes which blind the man." — (Blind) Master Po

Perhaps this show's most powerful and enduring imagery appeared in its opening minute. Here the audience was privy to a flashback of young Caine in the Shaolin temple, a sequence that quickly summarized his educational process— the ritual shaving of his head, and his excruciatingly painful rite of passage back into the everyday world.

Like Caine's Chinese priests, the drill sergeants of the United States Marine Corps require shaved heads of their new arrivals in boot camp— ostensibly for hygienic purposes, but also to instill a democratic sameness among their new enlistees. New Marine recruits, like Buddhist novices, absorb their indoctrination in an arguably cult-like setting in which one's pre-existing ego is thoroughly subjugated to a higher calling.

While voluntarily allowing one's head to be shorn is a gesture of submission, involuntary and sudden baldness can feel downright humiliating. Having received my first infusion of follicle-killing

71

chemotherapy drugs, I would soon be bald. But rather than allow my perfectly good head of thick, salt-and-pepper hair to slowly whither and fall out, we would preemptively remove it, Andrea and I had agreed.

During my thus far brief familiarity with the field of oncology, I had come to understand that being touched by cancer permanently alters one's existence, necessitating a lifetime of prudent medical surveillance and healthful lifestyle changes. Once thus touched, it is as if the cancer patient has been beckoned across a terrifying and special threshold, from which there can be no return.

I have never quite cared for the term "survivor" as applied to former cancer patients. As a former smoker who had "quit for good" and then relapsed on numerous occasions, I understood that one was never truly an "ex-smoker" until he entered the afterlife. Likewise, cancer is a cunning and resilient enemy, largely immune to absolute, permanent defeat and thus capable of renewing hostilities at any time. At what arbitrary milestone can one justifiably declare victory? It seems logical to me that one could not be definitively described as a "cancer survivor" until he has perished from something else. And yet we veterans of combat with this cruel and lethal adversary have certainly earned the right to our own category, a label that distinguished us from the general population.

On the morning of Sunday, June, 1, 2008, while taking my place for this ceremonial shearing, I conjured up a new term, one that seemed to me a more accurate description than "survivor." As Andrea and June applied the scissors and the razor, I decided that I would be formally joining the "Order of the *Canceroids*."

* * * * * * * * *

We set up my chair in June's backyard, the better to leave my hair to the birds for nest-building. I should point out that this type of coiffure requires no particular hairstyling skills... one needn't be a master carpenter, after all, in order to burn a house to the ground. As June and my new bride playfully cut away, I watched my hair fall to the ground and felt increasingly naked.

"You're gonna hear this a lot," said June, "So let me be the first— you have a really nice-shaped head!" How many times must she have heard this lame attempt at a compliment? Andrea wholeheartedly agreed with June... but then, she had always had a thing for bald men. After we finished, I immediately covered my bare scalp with a pirate's doo-rag. Despite Andrea's apparent Kojak complex, she bought me three more such head coverings. One or another them would remain in place, even as I made love and slept, for five months.

I felt increasingly sleepy as we drove from Spencertown to Saratoga, and snoozed in one of Sarah's living room easy chairs for most of Sunday afternoon. When I awoke, I was surprised for an instant to find myself bald. It was going to take me a while to get used to this, I could tell. Unfortunately, I would have plenty of time. I reported for work on Tuesday in my doo-rag, and I immediately realized how drastically my world had changed as the comments from customers began—

"Gee, your hair is really short."

"Aren't you a little early for Halloween?"

"New summer hairdo?"

To be fair, it might have been because I was relatively young and healthy-looking for an oncology patient, and it didn't occur to such customers that the long claws of cancer might ever reach someone like me. Now, these comments didn't really bother me at all, but I sensed varying degrees of impropriety in such inquiries. Even before I was diagnosed with cancer, I had been aware that quite a few chemo-bald customers passed through Guido's in a given week, and I would never have dared to so invade *their* privacy.

Among males, one often associates total baldness with outsized characters such as professional wrestlers, Bond villains, and chefs. Among women, however, baldness is uniformly freakish, and there can be but few explanations. The courageous French citizens who participated in the Resistance during World War II reserved a special punishment for their women who had slept with the German occupiers— shaving their heads and then parading them through the streets of Paris. Today, female baldness strongly suggests cancer. Unlike men, women who lose their hair to chemotherapy automatically lose their anonymity as cancer patients. For those women who have thus lost their beautiful locks in the wake of extensive breast cancer surgery, the multiple humiliation must surely be more devastating than I or any other man is capable of comprehending.

There was an unwritten etiquette to cancer, I had perhaps long known but now fully appreciated. One mustn't inquire about such things, even of an acquaintance, unless invited to do so through some sort of subtle social clue. However, now that I was chemo-bald myself, it was acceptable for me to initiate a sympathetic conversation with a fellow Canceroid. Furthermore, I felt a responsibility to uphold this code, to vigilantly maintain the "Etiquette of the Order" that I had just joined. And so I quickly formulated a concise response to inane or inappropriate questions about my hair, one that gently but unambiguously corrected the transgressor—

"I HAVE CANCER," I would reply with a polite smile as I portioned their salmon or pointed out a new floor stack of Pinot Noir.

"I… I'm so sorry," they would typically stammer.

"I'm not!" I would reassuringly respond. "Hodgkin Lymphoma is very treatable, and I'm getting great care right here in the Berkshires." Besides, I would usually add, I was now married to Andrea… on balance I was having a great year.

My hairlessness confirmed to many of my customers the rumors that they had already heard, and so I sometimes attracted an entirely different sort of attention during my months of baldness, something I welcomed. On these occasions I was discretely approached by other BHO patients, fellow Canceroids in need of a little fellowship and comfort. Our little conversations made us both feel better.

Having taken it upon myself to identify and uphold these nebulous standards of cancer etiquette, I must confess to accidentally discovering in my own conduct another sort of code violation—

Gentlemen, next time you happen to be introduced to a woman and learn that she is a breast cancer "survivor," be careful to firmly hold her gaze for a moment. What I call the "subconscious breast cancer boob-check," a quick glance to her torso with an involuntary *are those things real?* inquisitiveness, is a surprisingly common impulse that would best be stifled.

* * * * * * * *

Just as the swallows reliably return to Capistrano every March, one's hair grows back after chemotherapy. "It'll come back nicer than before," several veteran Canceroids assured me, beginning with June. But I was especially encouraged to recall that the mighty Samson himself managed to grow *his* hair back. Shortly thereafter he was again physically powerful, strong enough to dislodge the giant supporting pillars beneath the roof of the Philistine's temple and kill thousands more of the enemy before perishing himself in the collapse.

Like Samson's empowering mane, my hair would eventually return, I knew. But although my baldness would be temporary, I had permanently joined the Order of the Canceroids. It wasn't that long ago that being thus touched was an express ticket to the cemetery. However, during my lifetime cancer has evolved from a virtual death sentence into almost a rite of passage… a life-altering process not unlike surviving a tour of duty in the Marines, becoming a monk, or even completing a grueling ergometer race. Those who have endured the ordeal, the self-described survivors, are visible all around us, hosting their fund-raising walks and sporting their awareness-raising pink ribbons.

I was still a novice Canceroid, and I was far more concerned with getting through my treatments than with calling attention to my illness. Being so new at all of this, I had no idea just how much unsolicited advice I was about to attract.

FLOWER POWER AND HARD SCIENCE

Hair loss... weight loss... nausea... exhaustion... the side effects of chemotherapy treatments have long been fairly familiar to most people. Immediately after my chemo infusions began, however, I discovered that there was another consequence of cancer that no one had ever warned me about.

It would usually arise like this— a well-meaning acquaintance or customer would comment upon my absence of hair, and I would (somewhat) politely inform him that I had cancer. He would then proceed to tell me about his cousin's co-worker who knew someone whose sister-in-law had cured her malignancy by ingesting some secret herbal cure... bark tea, or some such crud. "It boosts your body's *natural healing powers*," he would typically go on to explain. "Oh— and you also oughta get yourself some magnets to help re-align your *energy field*." Or something like that. The big pharmaceutical firms didn't want us to know about these things, of course, because they make trillions of dollars every year selling their cancer drugs. The last thing they would want is an actual cure.

These well-meaning folks were demonstrating in their own way their heartfelt compassion and concern, I knew. Might they also be onto something that I should know more about?

I am definitely not a complete naysayer about unproven, "alternative" science. In the early 1980's, for example, I resorted in frustration to such remedies for my severe allergies. After my sudden and seemingly complete cure, I had little choice but to credit my homeopathy despite its completely unscientific foundations and dismal track record in blind studies. Likewise, during my career in the wine trade I have become convinced of the value of "biodynamic" viticulture, a variant of organic farming rooted in mysticism and cosmology. For whatever reason, many biodynamic wines— too many for me to dismiss as coincidence— have impressed my professional palate with an extra dimension of flavor. Biodynamic wines often seem blessed with a special vibrancy, something that might suggest to the fancy-minded that the vintner has somehow captured and bottled the essential life-force of both vine and soil. Closer to both my home and my particular illness, my Berkshire neighbor Kathy R. credibly claims to have attained a full remission from her stage IV Hodgkin Lymphoma after receiving injections of "714X." This unapproved anti-cancer treatment has never survived any rigorous sequence of mainstream scientific examination.

Based on these and other experiences, I appreciate that not everything related to living human beings or our experiences can be explained by science alone. In other words, science has no business claiming a monopoly on the truth.

Science, of course, begs to differ.

As evidence of science's intellectual primacy, some academics smugly cite the Catholic Church's persecution of the Italian mathematician Galileo Galilei (1564-1642) for promulgating his methodically reasoned conclusion that the sun— rather than our planet Earth— was the center of our solar system. They delight in describing his 1633 Inquisition, in which he was accused of heresy and threatened with torture unless he recanted his views... and how his predecessor Giordano Bruno had been similarly tried and then burned at the stake in 1600.

However, a fair-minded review of scientific history must also include instances in which new theories and discoveries were met with fierce, emotionally-charged resistance from within the scientific community itself. Notable examples of this include William Harvey (1578-1657), the first to accurately describe the nature of blood circulation; and Joseph Lister (1827-1912), a proponent of germ theory and antiseptic surgery. More recently, Dr. Sidney Farber (1903-1973) was initially ridiculed by his peers for suggesting in the 1940's that certain childhood leukemias were curable through chemotherapy. It often seems that in order to make the grade as accepted science, a novel concept must first survive scathing peer review often rooted in nothing more scientific than professional jealousy.

Whatever one's viewpoint, it is indisputable that science has been useful to mankind. In order to appreciate what makes it so, let's take a good look at its fundamental philosophical underpinnings.

On the overall time scale of life on Earth, science as we know it has a relatively short history. It was only four centuries ago— an eye-blink in human history, really— that Galileo concluded through repeated observations that falling objects accelerated toward the ground at a specific and consistent rate. By combining his observations of physical phenomena with a universally meaningful mathematical description, Galileo formulated a scientific theory that not only explained events that had already occurred, but also reliably predicted what would happen in the future under identical circumstances. What Galileo bequeathed us was more than just a single hypothesis that could be tested over and over again for validity. He encapsulated a system of thought for developing future scientific theories, a template for expanding our knowledge that would eventually extend the human reach to outer space and to cures for numerous horrible diseases.

This system of thought— this template— is known as the Scientific Method.

By design, scientific theories are *disprovable* rather than *provable*; that is, a million scientists might repeat Galileo's gravitation experiments and all arrive at corroborating results, but no amount of experimentation can ever transform his or anyone else's scientific theory into an absolute truth. To jump from *Galileo was right a million out of a million times* to *Galileo WILL be right ALL OF THE TIME* would be a leap of faith, though across an ever-narrowing gap with each experimental validation. And so, while one cannot absolutely prove a particular theory, one can indeed find substantial significance in a million failed attempts at disproving it. Yet one single experiment, if it were to go the other way, would essentially destroy the theory. Such hair-trigger "falsifiability" is the precarious existence of scientific theories. It has also become part of the test for separating "good science" from "junk science" in our society's supposedly preeminent crucible of truth, the American judicial system.

As forensic science progressed ever farther beyond the intellectual grasp of the average juror, "expert" courtroom testimony by hired-gun scientists of dubious impartiality began to increasingly sway juries in multi-million-dollar product liability cases. American jurisprudence scholars eventually recognized the need to establish and maintain standards of admissibility in court for purportedly scientific evidence. In the case of *Daubert vs. Merrell Dow Pharmaceuticals, 509 U.S. 579 (1993)*, the United States Supreme Court took the opportunity to define anew the threshold of admissibility for scientific evidence in federal court.

The *Daubert* petitioners had argued that their child's birth defects were directly caused by the mother's pre-natal use of a commonly used and FDA-approved anti-nausea medication. Their claim was backed by the usual "expert" testimony. The result of the case was a unanimous ruling that introduced a four-part "Daubert test" for acceptable science, a standard that closely reflected the intellectual framework of the Scientific Method—

1) Is the evidence based on a testable theory or technique?
(In other words, is the theory in question FALSIFIABLE?)

2) Has the theory or technique been peer reviewed?
(i.e., Has it been subjected to and survived academic and/or professional scrutiny by those best qualified to expose its fallacies or errors?)

3) In the case of a particular technique, does it have a known error rate and standards controlling the techniques of operation?
(i.e., Is the experiment REPEATABLE in that everyone is performing it according to the same set of scientific standards?)

4) Is the underlying science generally accepted?
(i.e., Are the underlying mechanisms and/or cause-and-effect relationships widely acknowledged by the scientific community?)

What sort of cancer treatments pass muster with Galileo's Scientific Method and the Supreme Court's *Daubert* test? As it stood in the first decade of the twenty-first century when I was undergoing my treatments, the vast majority of cancer patients faced the stark reality that the only scientifically supported, government-approved paths to their cure usually involved one or more invasive, onerous therapies— surgery, chemotherapy, and/or radiation. (Other cutting-edge modalities were just beginning to appear on Big Science's horizon... more on those in a later chapter.)

It has long been human nature to seek ever-easier solutions to our problems— weight loss without dieting or exercising; instant spiritual fulfillment from TV pop psychology; and the treatment of cancer with some obscure plant extract that magically "energizes the body's own natural cancer-fighting powers." Surf the Internet for "cancer cures," and one finds an astonishing array of such postings.

One of the most popular alleged folk cures for cancer available on-line is "Essiac tea," an apparently miraculous potion discovered by a Canadian nurse named Rene Caisse. ("Essiac" is her surname spelled backwards.) Nurse Caisse supposedly learned of this preparation from the indigenous *Ojibway* people in the Province of Ontario. Here one might curiously observe that miracle plant-based medicines seem to originate in faraway exotic places, or at least among exotically foreign people... why are they never developed by, say, autoworkers in Detroit, or corn farmers in Iowa?

Essiac tea is a blend of several botanicals— slippery elm inner bark, Indian burdock root, rhubarb root, and sheep sorrel. Formulas vary, depending on the source. Some include a total of eight different plant extracts. And while Nurse Caisse had reported cures of hundreds or even thousands of seriously ill cancer patients during the early- to mid-1900's, the fine print on one of the "official" Essiac websites (essiacinfo.org) speaks for itself—

> *No extensive clinical studies have been performed as yet which* (sic)
> *would provide conclusive evidence that Rene Caisse's herbal formula*
> *will alleviate, cure or prevent any disease or condition. The purpose of*
> *this site is to provide historical information about Rene M. Caisse and*
> *the history of Essiac. All excerpts were taken from documented sources.*

Want a second opinion? Memorial Sloan-Kettering Cancer Center (MSKCC) in Manhattan is, like Boston's Dana-Farber, one of the top five cancer hospitals in the United States. In the mid 1970's, MSKCC tested both dried and liquid samples of Essiac in a series of experiments on mice. They concluded that Essiac did not make the immune system more active, nor did it act as an anticancer drug. Researchers at MSKCC tested Essiac again in the early 1980's and found in it no anti-cancer activity in numerous studies.

In 1999, MSKCC established its Integrative Medicine Service in order to complement its mainstream medical services as well as to scientifically examine the purported cancer-fighting properties of alternative therapies such as herbal remedies. Regarding Essiac, MSKCC's Integrative Medicine Service web page notes that *"Despite insufficient clinical evidence, many cancer patients use Essiac tea as an alternative treatment based on anecdotal evidence."*

Throughout these extensive scientific studies, Essiac was found to be more or less harmless— although it appeared to actually *promote* breast cancer development in some studies. But useless, "harmless" remedies such as Essiac are in fact quite dangerous when their disingenuous or downright deceitful advertisements dissuade otherwise treatable cancer patients from seeking therapy that has been scientifically established as actually effective. The tragic reality that unproven herbal remedies and alternative therapies can actually kill people is perhaps best illustrated by the notorious Laetrile Affair of the 1970's.

The purportedly anti-cancer drug Laetrile was a semi-synthetic compound that was derived— like cyanide— from almonds and/or apricot pits. It was generally dismissed as useless by the medical profession and widely outlawed throughout the United States during the 1950's and '60's. However, in the face of a possibly fatal illness, it is understandable that many cancer patients might be seduced by the possibility of an easy cure. In the 1970's, quite a few of them sought out and were able to receive Laetrile treatments in neighboring countries.

In October of 1977, seven-year-old Joseph H. of Saratoga County, New York was diagnosed with Hodgkin Lymphoma. His family physician recommended standard oncological care— a regimen of surgery, radiation, and perhaps chemotherapy that at the time could claim an 85% successful cure rate. But after Joseph's parents considered the surgical horrors of their young son's prescribed staging laparotomy and likely spleen removal, they instead whisked him off to Jamaica, where Joseph received what was billed as "metabolic therapy" as well as injections of Laetrile.

When Joseph H. and his family returned home in November of 1977, the office of the New York State Commissioner of Health and Social Services charged his parents with neglect for failing to avail themselves of mainstream medical care for their minor child. The State of New York initiated legal proceedings to remove Joseph H. from his home and have him treated according to the prevailing standard of care. A judge on loan from the local District Court presided over the hearing before a packed Saratoga County courtroom.

Judge Loren Brown was no stranger to Hodgkin Lymphoma. As the trial began, a close friend of his had two daughters undergoing treatment for HL. Judge Brown also had considerable respect for orthodox western medicine and all it had accomplished during his lifetime. But because the "burden of persuasion" rested upon the State of New York, all Joseph's parents needed to do was demonstrate to Judge Brown that Laetrile, which in fact had been outlawed in New York, was viewed favorably as a course of cancer treatment by at least one New York-licensed physician.

Under the prevailing family law statues in June of 1978, Judge Brown, despite his private misgivings, had no choice but to side with the parents.

82

His decision was affirmed by the New York Supreme Court in November of that year, and Joseph H. died of his Hodgkin Lymphoma in 1980. Many other Laetrile recipients died along with him, either from their untreated cancers or, in some cases, from cyanide poisoning.

With the advantage of hindsight, the parents' choice of a course of treatment that virtually guaranteed Joseph's death is difficult to comprehend. How could it be possible that two loving, intelligent parents had fallen for the false promise of an unproven, illegal drug over the 85% chance offered by conventional therapy? Maybe they were terrified... or perhaps they were torn between the conflicting opinions from actual doctors, and opted for what they thought would be the easiest path for their son.

In the annals of fraudulent miracle treatment, Laetrile has plenty of company. Beginning in 1977, Dr. Hollace S., a musicology Ph.D., was twice diagnosed with Hodgkin Lymphoma. On both occasions she achieved remissions via standard chemotherapy. When her cancer appeared a third time, she turned to a controversial New York cancer doctor who prescribed coffee enemas and other unproven treatments. Professor S. perished from HL in 1995 at the age of 40.

As I reviewed these and similar cases, I was amazed at what some apparently normal, high-functioning people were actually capable of believing. There were those— especially in my immediate Berkshire County vicinity, it seemed— who are convinced that every single thing our government or mainstream press tells them is a lie. And yet somehow many of these same people uncritically accept as truthful the numerous outrageous and completely unsubstantiated governmental conspiracy theories regarding the 9/11 attacks, the allegedly intentional spread of AIDS, and about Big Medicine's suppression of alternative cancer cures.

Why are people so willing to believe such things without a shred of proof? Perhaps, as the journalist Henry Louis Mencken once opined, the average citizen is tempted to blame his misfortunes on large and unseen forces conspiring against him, rather than accept his limitations and life's vicissitudes at face value. But the very same logical loophole that perpetuates conspiracy theories simultaneously disqualifies them as useful hypotheses... it all goes back to a basic tenet of the Scientific Method.

Conspiracy theories survive and seemingly linger indefinitely among the larger population precisely because they are by definition impossible to falsify, as one cannot prove a negative. It cannot absolutely be proved that the CIA *didn't* blow up the World Trade Center or invent AIDS; nor, either, that the giant pharmaceutical firms *aren't* hiding from the public a known cancer cure. To make matters worse, any attempt to refute such theories with reason and facts tends to energize those who equate the gentlest counter-argument with conspiratorial suppression. Moreover, there's good money to be made from bad science, and so medical charlatans and junk science hucksters readily prey upon those whose reasoning powers are compromised by scientific naïveté, fear, and/or a reflexive distrust of officialdom.

This is why there will always be outrageous, foundationless conspiracy theories, and why there will always be a market for false cancer remedies like bark tea and Laetrile.

* * * * * * * * *

In the final analysis, hard science is our only reliable tool for understanding our human experiences in such a way that we might make advantageous use of them in the future. It is our only means of distinguishing between legitimate medicine and useless or downright fraudulent medicine. It follows that the Scientific Method— in the form of controlled clinical trials— provides the only way to distinguish promising botanical cures from the profusion of worthless treatments shamelessly marketed to cancer patients, those unfortunate folks whose otherwise sound judgment might understandably be compromised by a sense of desperation. After all, when one's oncologist resignedly admits after a long and hard-fought battle that medical science can offer nothing further, then any unproven treatment— from Laetrile to bark tea to coffee enemas— might seem well worth exploring.

Fortunately for mankind, there will always be new, previously unimagined discoveries. We should strive to balance healthy scientific skepticism with a mind open to fresh and original ideas. At the frontier in the war on cancer, for example, targeted molecular therapy is taking the battle right down to the very building blocks of matter. Likewise, immunotherapy— the induced stimulation of the patient's own immune system to attack cancer cells— is currently showing promise... not unlike so many herbal cures that claim to "boost the body's natural healing mechanisms." As for the medicinal use of herbs and other botanicals, the língzhī (or reishi) mushroom, which has been used for thousands of years in the Far East, shows genuine therapeutic potential. Contemporary studies suggest that it is indeed useful as an anti-cancer medication, although its mechanism is still not completely understood.

I suppose that one's choice of treatment for cancer all comes down to one's comfort level. I "get" science. I understand and appreciate how our natural world works; I comprehend the laws governing the interactions of everything from protons to planets. I do realize, however, that not everyone shares my child-like fascination with the mathematical elegance of orbits, or with the horrific mechanism of nuclear fission.

But as a scientifically minded person in the midst of chemotherapy, my patience was strained somewhat by those who spouted their completely unscientific suggestions about herbal cures and such. I delighted in telling them that my cancer was being treated with extracts of soil fungus as well as the colorfully blooming Madagascar periwinkle plant... the highest example, perhaps, of "flower power." I would then explain that these botanical compounds— Adriamycin, Bleomycin, and Vinblastine— were being used on me precisely because they had survived the necessary rigors of scientific testing and had proved themselves to be effective.

I appreciated that curing my cancer was going to take one hell of a lot of Big Science. But Big Science costs big money, and these well-tested, scientifically-proven medicines they were pumping into my veins were therefore quite expensive... far more costly than, say, a box of bark tea at our local co-op. In the world of Major League baseball, ace pitchers have been known to command eight-figure annual salaries. And so how much was it going to cost, I wondered, to have Dr. DeLeo mow down my Hodgkin Lymphoma?

BIG SCIENCE & BIG BUCKS
PART ONE

With so much time in bed after my increasingly debilitating infusions, the universe of cancer and its underlying science were mine to explore on my laptop. Andrea, quite naturally, hungered for information as well. Motivated by intellectual curiosity diametrically at odds with my physical exhaustion, my wide-eyed fascination with Big Science took me down some unexpected paths. I share here what I think are some interesting and significant aspects of the war between science and cancer.

Note to potential plaintiffs— I am not a cancer researcher, but I can understand and accurately summarize what I read. Everything in this chapter has been meticulously gleaned from reputable medical journals and newspaper articles. If you find yourself waxing litigious because of something I have written, I will happily refer you to the appropriate defendant.

* * * * * * * *

As early America's whale oil street lamp and horse-drawn carriage yielded to technological advances in electricity and mechanization, Western Civilization's medical classes concurrently directed their increasingly science-based methodologies against mankind's deadliest afflictions. By the dawn of the twentieth century, the era of well-schooled and well-meaning "doctors" actually doing more harm than good was finally over. It had begun to appear that every disease known to befall the human race would be treatable by some clinically-proven fungal extract or synthetic compound. However, twentieth-century medical researchers gradually figured out that cancer differed greatly from ailments caused by a virus or bacterium. There was no cancer "germ" to seek and destroy, and therefore no lone scientist was going to isolate its antitoxin at his personal laboratory bench and claim individual credit. Conquering cancer was going to require a lot of Big Science.

A noteworthy measure of mankind's commitment to cancer's defeat is the number of Nobel Prizes thus far awarded for accomplishments beneficial to its cure, like battle ribbons conferred for small victories within a larger war. If one includes those for peripheral discoveries ranging from CT-scan technology to the advances in physics that enabled radiotherapy, then the war on cancer can arguably claim thirty-three out of the five-hundred-forty laureates in the sciences between 1901 and 2008. In contrast, research into diphtheria, lupus, typhus, tuberculosis, and yellow fever yielded only single medallions; malaria and diabetes, a pair each. But Nobel-worthy Big Science costs Big Bucks, and therefore beating cancer was going to cost so much money that the involvement of the federal government was necessary.

In 1937, the United States Congress passed the National Cancer Institute Act, founding an eponymous research and development organization (NCI) devoted to curing cancer. They modestly funded it with an initial yearly appropriation of $400,000— about $6 million worth of inflation-adjusted 2009 dollars. NCI merits considerable credit for fostering the development of dozens of chemotherapy drugs during the decades immediately following World War II. Thanks to NCI's support and encouragement, Big Science was able to tally a few early and clear-cut battlefield successes (dare one say *cures*?) over certain types of lymphoma and leukemia.

And yet, as the dawn of the 1970's marked the thirty-third anniversary of NCI's optimistic establishment, a singular, definitive answer to cancer— if any such thing in fact existed— still lay beyond Big Science's lavishly financed reach. This was a discouraging parallel, in a sense, to Albert Einstein's fruitless, four-decade quest for the elusive "unified field theory" with which he had hoped to elegantly explain every physical phenomenon in our universe. But America in the 1970's was still a "can-do" country.

Justifiably bullish about America's scientific capabilities following

NASA's spectacular 1969 lunar conquest, President Nixon shortly thereafter signed the National Cancer Act of 1971, substantially escalating what was first openly described at the time as the "war on cancer." NCI's budget quadrupled over the next five years, providing fresh billions in research funds in order to fulfill, it was widely hoped and expected, the nation's quest for cancer's cure in time for its two-hundredth birthday.

In retrospect, however, America's contemporaneous nightmare in the swamps of Vietnam might have been a more appropriate model than her space program, as cancer thenceforth proved as implacable an enemy as the Viet Cong, the effort to overtake it as indecisive and seemingly open-ended. By the mid-1970's, as the American Bicentennial approached, the Vietnamese conflict had dissipated into a murky non-victory while the "war on cancer" raged on without a visible endpoint.

As with America's post-Vietnam military budget, her river of cancer dollars continued to flow perforce over the next few decades, accelerated by the periodic welling of public sympathy so naturally extended toward the disease's unfortunate victims. On autumn's first Saturday of 1998, for instance, thousands of Canceroids noisily gathered in our nation's capital to lobby for even more research funding. Congress, in response, cranked wider yet the federal treasury's floodgate, understandably reluctant to deny sloganeering, chemo-bald protesters the additional tax dollars that were Washington's to allocate.

While these past seven decades' worth of federally underwritten research has indeed wrought some tangible and valuable results, Americans have been conditioned by history to expect grand slams from their government's grand efforts. After all, with less than a decade of research and development, the Manhattan Project had hatched the mushroom clouds that closed out World War II. Twenty-four years later, NASA put human footprints on the moon within a similarly urgent time frame. But Big Science has thus far failed to hit cancer out of the park. And yet, as in a low-scoring diamond battle in which a bunt single might plate the winning run, Big Science's relatively tiny and incredibly expensive advances have constituted useful if hard-won progress... especially to people like me whose lives have been thereby spared or extended.

Congress, meanwhile, has kept the clamoring Canceroids at bay with more and more funding. In early 2009 they passed the 21st Century Cancer Access to Life-Saving Early Detection, Research and Treatment ("ALERT") Act, committing further talent and treasure to the anti-cancer cause while simultaneously demonstrating the importance of clever acronyms in our budgetary process. But just how worthwhile have been these seven decades of dedicated research, an estimated $200 billion in federal and private funding, and those thirty-three Nobel Prizes?

As I write this, by some measures Big Science has barely dented cancer. If one abstracts out the lives saved by early detection techniques for malignancies of the prostate, cervix, breast, and colon, then cancer's mortal toll appears to be barely diminished since the 1971 escalation of the "war" against it; barely changed, in fact, since 1950. And while Andrea and I are blubberingly grateful for Hodgkin Lymphoma's encouraging survival rates, a Stage IV pancreatic Canceroid planning the particulars of his imminent burial might understandably regard America's entire anti-cancer effort as a colossal, expensive waste. Meanwhile, the science itself is becoming exponentially bigger.

Big Science's inquiring eye began to probe the double helix for cancer's answer beginning in the 1970's, when NCI's annual budgetary swelling enabled new exploration into molecular genetics for novel therapies. Such research revealed that cells typically turn cancerous via a complicated intracellular messaging mechanism, as a secret wartime signal to blow up a critical bridge might be whispered from spy to spy through a sleeping city. Intercept and neutralize one of the operatives at the right time, and the sabotage is foiled. Likewise, reasoned the scientists, cancer might be arrested by synthesized compounds capable of disrupting its molecular pathway of enabling signals... a nice theory, albeit one that would require some *very* Big Science. However, with generous support from NCI's Molecular Targets Development Program, private companies began to produce exotic medical weaponry that would make James Bond or even the crew of the Enterprise envious as the pursuit of cancer increasingly resembled a high-tech chase on the big screen.

In 1976, an expert in recombinant DNA technology pooled his knowledge with the resources of a venture capitalist to incorporate the biotech firm Genentech, whose name they derived from a glib contraction of "Genetic

Engineering Technology." Genentech and its rivals are in the business of developing "targeted molecular therapy" drugs, the latest generation of anti-cancer treatments. These medicines are characterized by their Klingon-esque nomenclature as well as the high expectations of their signal-intercepting effectiveness.

Genentech won FDA approval in 1998 for HERCEPTIN® (Trastuzumab), a genetically re-engineered monoclonal antibody, part mouse and part human, that inhibits tumor growth two different ways— it flags wayward cells for destruction by the body's natural immune system, and it also disrupts the intercellular signal that causes them to over-reproduce. Genentech is responsible for other such "wonder drugs"— AVASTIN® (Bevacizumab) is another monoclonal antibody, approved in 2004, that intercepts the signaling protein necessary for "angiogenesis," the growth of the cancer cells' vital blood vessels. TARCEVA®(Erlotinib Hydrochloride), introduced in 2005, interrupts a signaling pathway in cells that would otherwise transform into a type of lung cancer.

Lest one conclude that Genentech has monopolized the molecular battlefield, in 2001 the Swiss pharmaceutical company Novartis introduced GLEEVEC®(Imatinib Mesylate), which targets the abnormal proteins that stimulate runaway growth of cells in chronic myeloid leukemia (CML) and certain gastrointestinal cancers. A Time magazine cover story in May of 2001 described GLEEVEC® as perhaps cancer's "magic bullet."

However, as the cancer research establishment has grudgingly learned over the decades since this "war" began, cancer can dodge bullets.

Innately programmed, seemingly, for self-perpetuation, cancer stealthily distributes its malevolent offspring throughout its human host, colonizing distant organs under the genetic equivalent of altered ID's to avoid detection and capture. Bent on defending themselves against medical attack, some cancer cells are actually capable of fashioning intracellular pump-like structures to purge themselves of chemotherapeutic toxins. And with a degree of intelligence that one might ascribe to invading extraterrestrials, cancer time and again outwits the molecular geneticists just when they think they have gotten a quantum step closer to a definitive cure.

Disrupt a cancerous colorectal cell's vascular supply lines with one drug, and it finds a way to nourish itself via redundant vessels. Interrupt a lung cancer cell's intracellular communications with another drug, and the cancer eventually recruits a backup transmitting enzyme. And while many CML and gastrointestinal cancer patients have extended their survival rates with targeted molecular therapy, their malignant cells tend to develop resistance to it within a few years.

Just as mankind's glimpses into fundamental physics via giant cyclotrons and telescopes haven't brought us much closer to an Einsteinian Unified Field Theory, Big Science's pursuit of the ultimate cancer cure through new and exotic medicine has so far been less than a smashing success. Perhaps the single greatest lesson learned from Big Science's quest for a *Star Wars*-like, high-tech cure has been that cancer is a very, *very* smart enemy, one that isn't going to disappear or surrender anytime soon.

* * * * * * * * *

But enough with the biochemistry and physics for now. As Elton John once sang, *"And all this science, I don't understand..."* Truth be told, I don't understand as much of it as I would like, either. No one does. No matter how far our scientists are able to advance mankind's understanding of the universe, it seems that there will always be a boundary, an imposing wall that separates us from nature's deeper mysteries. The war on cancer has certainly verified this, for the cure still lies beyond this barrier, awaiting the proper moment, perhaps, to be revealed to us. Meanwhile, we continue to combat cancer with the considerable body of science at hand.

It is understandably difficult for the average oncology patient to intuitively associate the medical science behind his cancer treatments with the curative process. Unlike, say, pain-numbing aspirin or throat-soothing lozenges, chemotherapy and radiation usher in physical misery rather than immediate relief from one's symptoms. It is natural, therefore, that a cancer patient might feel helpless and alone while undergoing all those PET- and CT-scans, chemical infusions, and zaps of radiation from such scary-looking equipment.

But somewhere between the hard science of space-age cancer warfare and the soft-headed "magicial herb" twaddle that so often dilutes New Age discourse into meaninglessness, there lies a middle ground, a readily accessible realm where many Canceroids have taken comfort and perhaps even improved their chances of survival.

It is human nature to grasp at any possible measure of personal control when confronted with adversity. In response to finding themselves under real or imagined attack, American civilians planted World War II "victory gardens" in their backyards, and then a decade later dug Cold War bomb shelters beneath them. Likewise, many Canceroids naturally wish to maximize their frightening odds by whatever means possible.

There is growing suspicion that more and more people are getting cancer because of two primary causes— synthesized chemicals in our environment, and diet of over-processed, chemically-raised (and preserved) foods. While in the short run we have precious little sway over the purity of our ambient air and water, we can exercise a measure of control over the food we ingest.

Despite its tremendous twentieth-century advances, mainstream western medical orthodoxy has been slow to recognize a relationship between diet and wellness. However, there have long been lone voices arguing otherwise. In the 1920's, the German-born Dr. Max Gerson (1881-1959) began to extol (as had Dr. Thomas Hodgkin a century before) the benefits of eating unprocessed natural foods. The "Gerson diet" consisted of raw vegetables and fresh organic juices, ostensibly to strengthen the body's immune system. In his later years, Gerson blamed industrial toxins in our foodstuffs for increasing cancer rates.

Shortly before his death, the Austrian scientist-mystic-philosopher Dr. Rudolph Steiner (1861-1925) presented his theory of "biodynamic agriculture," his approach to farming that eschewed artificial fertilizers and regarded the soil itself as an organism that must be nurtured and nourished in order to yield in return a healthful crop. Although Dr. Steiner's cosmological and mystical tenets of farming have yet to square with accepted science, it is difficult to find fault with a philosophy that recognizes a connection between human health and the vitality of the soil from which our diet arises.

Even Dr. Steiner's infamous fellow Austrian— he with history's most recognizable mustache— was a natural foods and anti-cancer crusader. Before taking up genocide in earnest, German Chancellor Adolph Hitler had adamantly advocated against smoking and for a more wholesome, natural diet in order to help reverse the high cancer rates of his rapidly industrializing nation. Like Hitler and Drs. Hodgkin, Gerson, and Steiner before him, Japanese-born George Ohsawa (1893-1966) promoted health through simple, natural eating.

Ohsawa revived notions of dietary balance from Greek antiquity as "macrobiotics," (literally "long life") which he introduced in America in the mid 1950's. Ohsawa's menu relied heavily on whole grains and beans with minimal meat... healthy, for sure, but macrobiotics also entailed a lifestyle philosophy so incongruous with Western folkways as to require a commitment extending well beyond one's food-shopping. However, many Americans maintain a chronic softness for anything esoteric and foreign, and thus elements of macrobiotics and other out-of-the-mainstream cuisines have regularly found their way into the stateside pantry, if only as a superficial cultural sampling.

As I endured my treatments and appointments during the summer of 2008, numerous superstar "wellness experts" regularly appeared in tabloids and on afternoon TV gabfests to promote their latest miracle foods... and, of course, their book sales. The public was listening, apparently. Foods high in anti-oxidants and Omega-3 oils had recently become *en vogue*. And as I personally witnessed at Guido's' seafood counter five or six days a week, many customers were demanding exclusively *wild* fish ("farmed" had become a profanity) caught no sooner than sometime that same morning.

I couldn't really get mad at so many otherwise intelligent and rational people for being a little neurotic about what they ate... it kept us in business, after all. But it seems to me that the "Rules for Staying Young" as set forth by Hall-Of-Fame Negro League pitcher Leroy Robert "Satchel" Paige (1906-1982) constituted nutritional and lifestyle advice as sensible— and probably just as scientific— as anyone else's:

1. Avoid fried meats, which angry up the blood.

2. If your stomach disputes you, lie down and pacify it with cool thoughts.

3. Keep the juices flowing by jangling around gently as you move.

4. Go very light on the vices, such as carrying on in society—
   the social ramble ain't restful.

5. Avoid running at all times.

6. Don't look back— something might be gaining on you.

There just might be something to this. If one reads between Paige's lines with a twenty-first century lens, it appears that he was recommending a healthy diet and a low-stress lifestyle. For what it's worth, whatever was gaining on Paige (it turned out to be heart trouble, not cancer) didn't catch the Hall of Fame Ace until a month before his seventy-sixth birthday.

My own rules for staying young and healthy included eating the foods that I love and that accordingly make me feel good. Although I have long been blessed with natural cravings for the usual "power foods" recommended by self-styled health gurus, such as salmon and broccoli, in the spirit of honesty I must also confess that my favorite, most soul-soothing chemo-day indulgence originated beneath the Golden Arches— a quarter-pounder with cheese, large fries with extra salt, and root beer. Proper nutrition could wait, I told myself. While I was undergoing cancer treatments, I would pamper my inner baby as much as possible.

In sharp contrast to my chemo-day fast food cravings, the common thread among the anti-cancer nutrition advocates seems to be a return to pure and natural simplicity in the form of food produced and packaged without artificial chemicals. Might this just be another kooky New Age fad? Mounting statistical evidence suggests otherwise.

Epidemiologists study illnesses as they affect populations, drawing conclusions by cross-referencing diseases with possible risk factors related to lifestyle, workplace conditions, and diet. Lyme Disease, for example, was identified because epidemiologists noticed an unusual concentration of childhood arthritis in a rural New England town. Rather than explain the precise biochemical mechanism of a particular cancer on the cellular level, epidemiologists correlate specific cancers with their likely causes— bladder cancer is frequently diagnosed among dry-cleaner employees who have worked with the solvent perchloroethylene, while mesothelioma arises almost exclusively in workers exposed to asbestos.

Synthetic chemicals are now everywhere around us, in our soil, water, air… and, often, in our food. Might the marriage of chemistry and cuisine— the artificial colors, flavors, preservatives, hydrogenated fats, and synthetic growth hormones that Americans regularly ingest— actually be a cause of cancer? Epidemiologists are finding patterns suggesting that they are… but they are also finding that the legal system is somewhat stacked in favor of Big Industry.

As explained in the previous chapter, the United States Supreme Court's 1993 *Daubert* definition of acceptable courtroom science bars unfounded, half-baked medical hypotheses from reaching the impressionable ears of jurors. Unfortunately, however, this *Daubert* standard can also shield the manufacturers of suspected carcinogenic compounds from accountability to the people they indirectly sicken and kill. This is possible because inferences from epidemiological data, self-evident though they might seem, often fare poorly under hostile cross-examination in the absence of corroborative "hard" science or a known underlying mechanism of cause-and-effect. Even before *Daubert*, however, it was behind the scant fig leaf of such scientific uncertainty that Big Tobacco and Big Industry successfully prolonged for decades their poison-for-profit enterprises.

And so I came full circle in my cancer self-education, in a way. Bigger and bigger science had taken us from whale oil and horse carriages to our present nano-digital era in little more than a century. But it is also true that our modern lifestyle— disinfected, deodorized, beautified, fertilized, and powered by all manner of synthesized chemicals— has come with an increasingly carcinogenic price tag.

Big Science has been extravagantly and expensively deployed against cancer for many decades now. It is thus another of life's great ironies that if Big Science were to probe long and deeply enough into the mysteries of cancer's causes, it might eventually see *itself* and the broad array of cancer-causing poisons it has pumped into our biosphere and bodies in the name of progress.

BIG SCIENCE & BIG BUCKS, PART TWO:
THE TALE OF TAXOL

With so much Big Science deployed in the war on cancer, naturally there are those who have profited handsomely from the effort, just like America's ship-builders during World War II and then her fighter-jet subcontractors during the Cold War. Troubling though this might be, it is important to recall that old-fashioned American patriotism alone probably couldn't have decided either conflict without benefit of the profit-driven supply channels of capitalism. Similarly, the war against cancer as thus far waged would have been impossible without rich people getting richer as a consequence.

I was extremely fortunate to have health insurance through my employer, coverage that paid for all of my medical expenses save for token, twenty-dollar co-payments upon each office visit. In total, my treatments would cost HMO Blue about $100,000... a few thousand for the surgery, a few thousand more for the radiation, and well over $50,000 for the chemotherapy and its related diagnostic procedures. This uneven ratio among the three modalities reflects the larger picture of cancer treatment. Oncopharmacology— i.e., cancer drugs— is big business. Accordingly, the world's giant pharmaceutical companies that manufacture drugs for chemotherapy and targeted molecular therapy often come under particularly harsh scrutiny for their sizable profit margins.

In theory, the cancer drug business seems pretty darn lucrative— synthesize a chemical compound that exhibits anti-tumor activity; patent it; test it on mice; get FDA approval; and then sit back as you and your stockholders become obscenely wealthy. But the giant pharmaceutical companies, organized as lobbyists in the halls of Congress as the "Pharmaceutical Research and Manufacturers of America" and colloquially known as "Big Pharma," argue that the enormous investment required to develop and gain FDA approval for a new drug, coupled with the relatively short window of profitable monopoly before its patent expires, are responsible for oncopharmacology's high price tags. Drug companies cite current development costs at around $800 million per drug. And while they enjoy twenty years of monopoly under current U.S. law before rival manufacturers are free to produce cheaper copycats, their patent's clock begins ticking before the time-consuming clinical testing begins.

Critics of Big Pharma rebut that much of the supposed cost of new drug development is borne by taxpayers through government-funded (NCI) research, while a significant portion of the remainder is spent on marketing and self-protective legal footwork rather than development. Whether the ultimate benefits of effective and widely available cancer treatments justify the sometimes murky co-mingling of public and private interests remains an open question, with valid arguments on either side.

Perhaps nothing better illustrates this controversy than the infamous Taxol Affair, a perfect storm of competing interests that inspired reams of federal legislation, provoked Congressional hearings over improper collaboration between Big Government and Big Pharma, and made a chemistry professor and his university unexpectedly rich. It even managed to foster the improbable allegiance of female cancer patients and big-bearded lumberjacks against the tree-hugging protectorate of the endangered Northern Spotted Owl.

* * * * * * * * *

The history of human medical practice is replete with discoveries of botanical-based healing agents, from myrrh (the soothing balm reportedly brought to Bethlehem by the Three Wise Men) to Penicillin. And yet, as cancer began to appear treatable in the late 1950's, very little was known about the potentially chemotherapeutic compounds originating in the plant kingdom. Secondary metabolites, by-products of plant physiology seemingly unrelated to the essential survival functions of most flora, have long been the basis of extracts useful to man such as dyes, perfumes, and a broad range of medicines. Might they also be a lush trove of anti-tumor agents? Big Science was anxious to find out.

Naturally bio-diverse environments— such as rain forests, including that of the Pacific Northwest— are rich with fabulously complex and potentially useful secondary metabolites. In 1960 the NCI research subdivision known as the Cancer Chemotherapy National Service Center (CCNSC) began to include botanical extracts among the materials they had been commissioned to test for possible cancer-fighting efficacy. During the next few years, CCNSC's initial studies of extracts drawn from the bark of the Pacific Yew tree (*Taxus brevifolia*) showed enough promise to justify further analysis. (Interestingly, the bark of the slippery elm— a component of Essiac tea— was apparently not included in CCNSC's botanical roundup. However, it was tested directly for anti-cancer activity by NCI in 1959 and again in 1970.)

The Pacific Yew, a coniferous cousin of pine, cedar, and spruce, grows in the shadows of the much taller, "old growth" timber native to Washington and Oregon. Yew had long been considered a "trash tree," worthless to lumbermen and useful only in such odd applications as outdoor decking, *faux*-primitive longbows, and canoe paddles. Whatever secret anti-cancer chemical it contained "*exhibited an unusually broad spectrum of anti-tumor activity*," according to a paper published by the medicinal chemist Dr. Monroe Wall for the one-hundred-and-fifty-third meeting of the American Chemical Society in 1967.

Dr. Wall off-handedly christened this newly discovered molecule "Taxol"— "tax-" in deference to the tree's formal botanical name, and "ol" for its operative alcohol appendages. Meanwhile, America's grassroots environmental movement— perhaps the greatest enduring legacy of the Woodstock Generation— was gaining strength as the sixties ended, generating noises that would soon reach the ears of Washington lawmakers.

Concern for the purity of America's air, water, and soil had already been codified into such legislation as the Federal Water Pollution Control Act of 1948 and the Clean Air Act of 1963. But the 200,000-gallon Santa Barbara oil spill of early 1969, an incident that played out for eleven days on nightly newscasts right beside the Vietnam coverage, gave impetus to a "save the planet" movement that readily dovetailed with the anti-war protests. Just as the big, bad Military-Industrial Complex was conveniently culpable in the minds of many for a needless war, Big Oil's blameworthiness for California's oil-drenched beaches seemed obvious. The first Earth Day was celebrated the following spring, and new environmental legislation suddenly sprouted in Congress. One such law was the Endangered Species Act of 1973, which extended federal protection to plant and animal species as well as *the ecosystems upon which they depend.*" And because the ecosystem of choice of the endangered Northern Spotted Owl was also home to the Pacific Yew, conservationists and cancer scientists suddenly found themselves on a collision course.

Studies at the Albert Einstein School of Medicine during the late 1970's suggested that Taxol worked by a previously unknown cytotoxic mechanism, preventing cell replication by inseparably binding microtubules. Researchers excitedly surmised that it might possibly prove effective against cancers that were unresponsive to their existing arsenal of chemotherapeutic weaponry. But further medical studies would become exponentially pricier as they graduated from mice to humans, and even more problematic would be the increasing pressure on Taxol's finite supply— four tons of Yew bark yielded scarcely more than an ounce of pure extract, a ratio equivalent to a single dose per tree.

Taxol entered Phase I trials in 1984 and Phase II trials a year later. The test results, released in 1988, were shocking— this derivative of the lowly Yew was a weapon of unprecedented effectiveness against ovarian cancer. Word quickly spread, and NCI was suddenly in need of 360,000 Pacific Yews per year to meet Taxol's anticipated demand. In response, the environmentalists dug in for battle. By the end of the 1980's, Taxol and the excitement surrounding it was beginning to exceed NCI's institutional capacity to manage its progression toward actual implementation. In order to continue the process of realizing Taxol's promise, NCI in 1989 exercised its existing provision for partnering with the private sector— a Cooperative Research and Development Agreement, or CRADA.

Bristol-Myers Squibb, the world's fourth largest pharmaceutical firm and known in corporate shorthand as B-MS, was selected from the quartet of applicants to assume the production, testing, and eventual distribution of Taxol. This was a perfectly reasonable transfer of assets and their attendant responsibilities from the government to the party best qualified to complete the project, according to one side of the debate. In the minds of critics, however, it was a huge and wholly undeserved windfall for a private company, an unprecedented giveaway of the American public's property.

In accordance with the CRADA's fine print, Bristol-Myers Squibb assumed sole possession of NCI's research to date as well as its entire existing stock of Taxol. While the contractual ink dried, B-MS quickly scrambled to avoid having to share its new asset with others, filing legal motions to hamstring potential rivals that might otherwise join them in bringing Taxol (or anything like it) to the market.

As a naturally occurring substance that had been in the public domain for over two decades, Taxol itself was unpatentable. But the short-term consequences of this inconvenience were neatly negated by a clause in the CRADA that granted Bristol-Myers Squibb an absolute five-year monopoly on Taxol. Furthermore, Taxol qualified as an "orphan drug." The Orphan Drug Act of 1983 empowered the FDA to incentivize the manufacture of relatively small amounts of drugs for rare diseases by granting drug companies profitable, absolute monopolies over them for seven years. (Ovarian cancer at that time fell a few thousand cases short of the 200,000-per-year legal threshold for a rare disease.)

Bristol-Myers Squibb even filed a slew of patent applications for the specific administration of Taxol for certain types of cancer, seemingly as one might attempt to patent the comforting service of chamomile tea for a head cold without any right of title to the herb itself. One can hardly blame them for this— under the provisions of the Hatch-Waxman Act of 1984, B-MS would be entitled as a patent holder to automatically deflect generic knock-offs of Taxol for thirty months at a time by simply filing lawsuits— whether meritorious or frivolous— against its would-be competitors. Finally, the firm also applied for and was controversially granted in 1992 a copyright for the drug's name, and thus did "Taxol" become TAXOL®(paclitaxel), the intellectual property, more or less, of Bristol-Myers Squibb. There remained, however, the nagging issue of supply.

Since the late 1960's the environmentalists had been agitating with stubborn determination. They successfully added the Northern Spotted Owl to the federal endangered list in mid-1990, and then halted all logging in national forests a year later with a court order. The lumber industry responded by claiming that such a ban would cost an estimated 30,000 jobs, nearly 18% of its workforce. Was the federal government putting a higher value on some goddamn bird than on the region's economy and the lives of cancer patients? Not exactly, for only the loggers were getting screwed on the owl's behalf. Under the Pacific Yew Act of 1992, Bristol-Myers Squibb had dibs on every Yew trunk standing in America's national forests. This law not only allowed the continued harvest of Yew trees from old-growth national forests, but also limited their sale to only those parties manufacturing Taxol... and under the terms of the CRADA, there would be no such party other than Bristol-Myers Squibb until 1998. But B-MS had known all along that there would never be enough Yew trees for it to bring their precious compound to the market...

The Taxol molecule would have to be synthesized.

Although numerous attempts were made in laboratories around the world, it was the Florida State University (FSU) chemistry professor Robert Holton who won the race to efficiently produce synthetic Taxol. And with a measure of business savvy not commonly associated with ivory tower academia, Professor Holton shrewdly claimed for himself and FSU the royalties for Taxol's as yet undiscovered chemical analogues that would surely arise in his laboratory over the next few years. Such foresight eventually enabled FSU to build a new science wing, and its star professor to do his traveling aboard his personal Gulfstream jet.

With the rights to Taxol securely within Bristol-Myers Squibb's grip and its future supply guaranteed, the new drug was fast-tracked through the FDA approval process and became available to cancer patients in 1993, thirty-one years after it first came to NCI's attention. Bristol-Myers Squibb's Taxol sales peaked at $1.6 billion in 2000, making it the most profitable cancer drug in history.

So many lingering questions have arisen from this affair; none, really, have been answered to everyone's satisfaction even after exhaustive

Congressional review. Might the development and implementation of Taxol have benefited more from competition between two rival companies than from a monopoly? Maybe… Immediately after being rebuffed, Rhône-Poulenc, the French pharmaceutical company that took second place in NCI's Taxol sweepstakes, began working on a Taxol analogue, suggesting that the market was big enough for more than one company. Might the federal government have imposed a windfall profits tax upon Bristol-Myers Squibb on behalf of the American people? In retrospect and in a perfect world, perhaps yes. However, imposing such a yoke up-front might have dissuaded B-MS as well as any other suitor from pursuing the CRADA in the first place.

Finally, one might rightly wonder whether gender politics might have further fueled this controversy. If Taxol had shown such initial promise against prostate or testicular cancer rather than a specifically feminine malignancy, might the nesting grounds of the Northern Spotted Owl have been deemed significantly more (or less) sacrosanct, and the impulse to defoliate them anymore or less justified?

Whatever one's conclusions about this Taxol Affair, or of the relationship in general between capitalism and medicine, the fact remains that the not-so-holy alliance of Big Science and Big Bucks ultimately succeeded in bringing an extremely useful anti-cancer treatment from tree bark to the chemo clinic. Taxol— or rather TAXOL®(paclitaxel)— has saved or extended the lives of many thousands of otherwise doomed Canceroids.

* * * * * * * *

As cancer continued its mortal harvest at a pace of over half a million lives annually— a toll equivalent to a daily Titanic— I was witnessing firsthand the battle to thwart it as waged on a regular basis at Berkshire Hematology & Oncology.

BHO is a private, for-profit corporation owned by four practicing oncologists, with a promising young doctor working his way into a fifth partnership position. Thus BHO functions much like a law firm, with partners, a non-equity associate, and about five dozen full- and part-time support personnel. The corporation recently purchased the 9500 square-foot building in which they have been a tenant since 1999. It is perhaps a revealing measure of cancer's increasingly significant role in our economy that the sale price— $2.1 million— amounted to fully one-third of the National Cancer Institute's entire 1937 budget, adjusted for inflation.

At its most fundamental, BHO is a retail purveyor of medicine. Just as I purchased wine for Guido's from wholesalers and then re-sold it to my customers at a mutually acceptable profit margin, BHO spends about $20 million per year on chemotherapy drugs and then administers them to its patients at a mark-up that covers its payroll and operating expenses. The typical profit margin on retail wine is 40-50% above cost; chemotherapy drugs are marked up at a far lower percentage. From such profits, American oncologists earn a median annual income of $262,000. Those in private clinics like BHO tend to earn more than that, while those in research-oriented facilities (such as Dana-Farber) tend to earn less.

Dr. DeLeo and his BHO colleagues earn excellent living wages— way more than the average American; more, even, than the average oncologist. And yet they earn far less than famous actors or rock stars, and a small fraction of what many professional baseball players take home. Those who vociferously rail against the profits related to cancer treatment might well ask themselves— the Yankees' Alex Rodriguez is paid half of an oncologist's annual salary *per game*... how many five-year remissions has he batted in? And Yankee closer Mo Rivera gets about two hundred grand *per inning*. Has he ever struck out cancer? Furthermore, one never hears of World Series victors sharing their wealth with their loyal fans; at least Bristol-Squibb Myers and its corporate ilk are owned by multitudes of stockholders who participate in the fruits of Big Pharma's profitable enterprises.

And so, with the meter running up a six-figure tab for the cure of my Hodgkin Lymphoma, my treatments progressed as the summer of 2008 unfolded. By my fifth chemotherapy treatment on Friday, July 25, my energy level had barely recovered from the fourth treatment two weeks prior. But I would need to put off my post-chemo crash until Sunday... I would need every last bit of strength in order to keep the important promise I had made back in January to work at the Williams College Football Mini-Camp all day on Saturday, July 26 as a kicking coach.

BERKSHIRE COUNTY FOOTBALL

The Berkshire region of western Massachusetts was as new to Andrea as our marriage. While we had attended school together in rural western New York, I was a Berkshire citizen by birth and had returned there soon after college. During the summer of our Chemo Honeymoon, I took it as my pleasurable duty to introduce my new bride to the finer aspects of my native realm. Tourist-oriented attractions were everywhere. And along with its self-described status as "America's Premier Cultural Resort," Berkshire County is also home to Williams College, a 2,000-student, private liberal arts college nearly as old as the republic itself.

Over the preceding two centuries, Williams College has enjoyed a strong tradition of academic excellence, annually sending hundreds of baccalaureates to America's most prestigious medical schools, law schools, and banking houses. It is consistently rated as one of the top two or three small colleges in the United States by U.S. News & World Report. In accordance with the Athenian notion of a "sound mind, sound body," Williams is also widely known for the excellence of its Division III athletic teams.

On Saturday, July 26, Williams head football coach Michael Whalen held his annual mini-camp. This was a shrewdly dual-purpose arrangement by which he sold priceless pigskin instruction to eager high school gridders as he simultaneously assessed their potential value to his roster. I had committed myself to working for the day as one of Coach Whalen's assistants back in January, when he had appeared at my Super Bowl eve wine tasting. However, I had undergone the fifth of my eight chemo infusions just the day before the mini-camp. Keeping this promise would be a challenge.

All NCAA head football coaches seem to share similar strains of gridiron DNA; only the balance varies. Some are shrewd blackboard tacticians who understand the interactions of their X's and O's with lucidity approaching mathematical genius. Tom Landry of the Dallas Cowboys in the 1960's and '70's is their archetype. Others, in the manner of Notre Dame's legendary Knute Rockne, are charismatic, natural-born motivators of their fellow men. Such coaches are often leather-lunged locker room orators, capable of inspiring imperfect human beings to somehow play beyond the mortal limits of their talent every Saturday.

Coach Michael F. Whalen might well have been destined at birth to assume his present station, for he is blessed with generous measures of both of these traits.

Upon observing this coach in person at my charity wine tasting, the comedian David Steinberg had commented that Hollywood could do no better at casting a college coach for filmdom. A former all-American offensive lineman, Whalen stands roughly the size of a Coke machine and speaks with a voice that seems to emanate from a very deep well. It is a combination that unambiguously communicates authority and strength. He is also a very smart man, not coincidentally a graduate of the same Division III college that produced New England Patriots coach Bill Belichick, the reigning NFL genius-in-residence.

Young Michael Whalen was training for a possible post-college playing career in the fledgling United States Football League when he was more or less recruited into the coaching profession by his former Wesleyan mentors. He simultaneously pursued graduate studies and a series of assistant coaching positions over the next few years, and eventually filled the prodigious footsteps of his Williams boss, the NCAA Hall of Fame coach Richard Farley. Whalen's tenure on the Williams sideline has been a seamless continuation of Coach Farley's many winning seasons.

Compared to big, obviously athletic men like Whalen and Farley, I don't look anything like a former football player to most observers, and they are approximately half right. I had been a kicking specialist in college, a football position whose uniqueness separates its practitioners behind a veil of intrigue. It also exposes them to the occasional scorn and ridicule of their teammates. But it is no wonder that regular players and coaches are often baffled by the role of such specialists. If kicking a football required pure brute strength, then the biggest, strongest player on the team would be the best kicker. This was never the case. Likewise, raw speed seemed to be an equally invalid determinant. And so, if kicking was a function of neither strength nor speed, what, exactly, was its essence? Was it something spiritual, or at least physically unquantifiable? Coach Whalen understood on some level that I knew the answer to such questions as he assigned me six young kickers to simultaneously instruct and assess that day at his mini-camp.

* * * * * * * *

I started kicking a football when I was six years old. In the early summer of 1965, my father moved us to the rural Wayne County town of Ontario. The houses in our new neighborhood were sparsely distributed, making new friendships difficult to form. Whether by divine providence or random fate, I stumbled upon a yellow plastic football during one of my lonely wanderings in the vast open field behind our new home. With so few neighborhood playmates, I made up games to play by myself—seeing, for instance, the minimum number of kicks necessary to get my ball to the other end of the meadow.

I soon joined my father on autumn Sundays as he sat transfixed in front of the television all afternoon, rooting for his New York Giants. Although it took me a couple of seasons to understand the game, I could still see that the NFL players were big and fast and strong… everyone but the *kickers.* By comparison they seemed like everyday men, physically unimposing. And yet their talent was so obvious as footballs practically leaped from their insteps and sailed up through the air as if weightless. In the late 1960's an influx of European soccer players joined the NFL and co-opted the vast majority of the kicking positions. When five-foot-eight, one-hundred-seventy-pound Garo Yepremian of Cyprus came to prominence with the Super Bowl champion Miami Dolphins, I finally had a diminutive left-footed kicker to idolize and emulate.

By seventh grade I was living in a parallel universe of my own creation. A good two years behind my classmates in physical development, it was clear that I was unsuited to interscholastic athletic competition. I was small-framed, slow of foot, and not especially coordinated. But I had my football, and also a bicycle that steadily muscularized my legs as it transported me to vacant fields. There, in meditative solitude, I honed my chosen art for hours and years on end.

Insofar as Andrea knew me back then, she never had any reason to understand that kicking was my sacred and precious refuge. Soccer and basketball were our high school's prestige sports; Wayne Central didn't even have a football team. But I knew that I might well become good enough to eventually kick for a small, Division III college, and I pretty much focused all of my efforts in that direction at the expense of academics and a social life. My efforts paid off. A couple of years after graduating from Wayne Central, I was named the starting punter and kicker at Union College in Schenectady, New York.

My best season came in 1979. That magical autumn began with a field goal against Wesleyan freshman Michael Whalen in a preseason game, and ended when I sent a penalty-shortened kickoff through the uprights from midfield to the drunken roars of my fraternity brothers. In between, I punted sixty-six times in eight games; converted seventeen of my twenty-two placekick attempts; recovered a fumble on a kickoff; connected on a forty-seven yard field goal; and even managed to draw a flagrant facemask foul while making a touchdown-saving tackle. All told, I was primarily responsible for two-thirds of our team's victories that year. The following spring, I further refined my craft on Union's rugby field.

By devoting so much thought and energy to becoming a college kicker absent much in the way of natural talent, I concurrently accumulated a significant body of knowledge about the subject, wisdom that was no longer of any utility after college. I wanted to share it with any interested parties whom it might actually benefit, and the venerable edifices of Williams College stood just a few short miles away when I moved back to the Berkshires in the late 1980's. Thus did I come to spend a few seasons as Williams' unpaid and unofficial kicking instructor, until circumstances took me to the other end of Berkshire County, too far from the campus to continue in this capacity.

When Coach Farley stepped down in 2003, I wanted to help out his successor any way I could. Coach Whalen seemed like a kindred spirit, perhaps because we were close in age, or maybe because I had kicked my very first field goal against him. Though I was unavailable for daily team practice, I could certainly spare one day out of the summer for the annual mini-camp.

Coach Whalen and his mini-camp staff had prudently lined up back-up kicking coaches in case my cancer had rendered me unable to appear as promised. However, on the morning of Saturday, July 26, I punctually arrived at the Williams College practice fields, half-flummoxed by the chemotherapy drugs from the day before and thankfully still buzzing with the steroids that would enable me to remain upright for the duration of the day.

The mini-camp was a day-long affair, split into morning and afternoon sessions just like a typical day in college pre-season. The hundred or so participants, all on the verge of their high school senior seasons, would thus get an appetizing glimpse of college athletic life. On Coach Whalen's whistle they divided according to position, ready to participate under their assigned coaches in a long sequence of drills and tests. My particular area of expertise lay in converting high school place-kickers into college place-kickers.

Under high school rules, a kicker may use a two-inch tee for field goal and extra point attempts, while college kickers are required to kick the ball held directly on the ground, as in the NFL. The transition is more difficult than one might expect, as one's steps and body placement require extensive reconfiguration. I myself never had to make these adjustments until I started coaching many years after the end of my career, as college rules also allowed the tee until 1989. But I was able to systemize the necessary changes into an easy-to-demonstrate process that would immediately allow my kicking students to productively practice the necessary method on their own... without the usual trial-and-error process.

* * * * * * * * *

Back when I played football at Union College, I had always been too focused on my kicking to develop my understanding of the game as a whole. I came to regret this laziness on my part, especially after watching enough of Williams College football practices and games to understand that they were running NFL-caliber plays and schemes, only with smaller and less-speedy athletes. ("These are the smartest college students in the *country*," Coach Farley used to boast. "We can teach'em anything we want!")

A kicking specialist focused solely on his craft might also fail to recognize that the game of football is conducted much like a military conflict, with a similar degree of importance placed upon scouting the enemy and preparing a detailed battle plan. On a typical Saturday during the Williams football season, Whalen and his nine assistants have collectively spent a hundred hours during the preceding week analyzing three games' worth film of their opponent, identifying their strengths, weaknesses, and tendencies. They have devoted three afternoons of practice time leading their starting offense against a "scout team" of second-string defenders emulating the opponent's formations; likewise, the Williams starting defense has faced a scout team posing as the enemy offense. As would an NFL team, Coach Whalen's Ephs enter every game as thoroughly prepared as practicable.

In order to help me better understand the decision-making processes on the sideline, a few days after the mini-camp I asked Coach Whalen to talk me through a hypothetical game situation— Williams has the ball, third down and four to go at its own forty-yard line in the fourth quarter of a close game. The ball has just been positioned for play by the officials, and Whalen has just twenty-five seconds to decide how to proceed and then communicate his commands to his eleven players on the field.

As the valuable seconds tick away, Whalen consults his coaches in the observation booth for input. ("A very short conversation," laughed Whalen. "Not a panel discussion!") Does one run or pass in a third-and-four situation? It's generally a toss-up. If Whalen decides to run, he calls the play himself. If instead he chooses to pass, he will turn to his quarterback coach for a suggested play. Now he has to get the call into the huddle and get the play off in time.

Football plays are codified in an arcane language. One of Williams' simple running plays, for example, is named "*Rip Stud 40 Counter.*" Whatever this means, it conveys enough precise information so that all eleven players on the field know exactly what to do. If Whalen chooses to call such a play, he will typically relay it to the huddle on the lips of a substitute wide receiver. However, if Whalen decides upon a more complex play that might lose something in the translation— such as "*Track to Right Near Y Lucky Drift Right Throwback Strike*"— he will signal a two-digit number to his quarterback, who wears a special wristband with an indexed menu of such verbosely-titled plays. The Williams quarterback then repeats the play in the huddle, and then the Ephs come to the line and execute the play… ideally with a degree of precision commensurate with their many hours of practice.

Whether or not Williams succeeds in gaining the necessary first-down yardage, Coach Whalen will have to make and communicate decision after pressure -packed decision to his players throughout the rest of the game. The head coach, staff, and athletes, therefore, actually comprise a high-tension, machine-like system for rapidly processing information and commands. It is easy to understand why kickers, who generally function separately from this sideline hurly-burly, are often marginal figures. All things considered, I'm glad I had been just a kicking specialist.

Coach Whalen's 2008 football mini-camp concluded with a giant, rah-rah huddle about an hour before sunset. What a splendid day this was! My kicking hip is so arthritic that it will probably require surgical replacement at some point, and yet I had been unable to resist booting a few field goals myself between drills. I went to bed that night deeply pleased that Andrea had finally been able to see me kick a football, able to observe firsthand this significant aspect of my makeup. She had also been able to hear eager young high school kickers as well as Williams staffers respectfully address me as "Coach May" in deference to the knowledge, talent, and experience that I had accumulated since my early youth. As I lay in bed, sunburned and my kicking bones a-throb, I finally began to feel the debilitating effects of the previous day's chemotherapy compounded by a long day of vigorous physical activity. It took little time to fall into a very deep sleep.

BERKSHIRE COUNTY MUSIC

Berkshire County has long been a convenient and desirable vacation destination for well-to-do New Yorkers. A mountainous spread of lakes, forests, and fresh air, it lies less than three hours north of Manhattan's chasms of masonry and glass. Fine arts venues tend to spontaneously sprout in such soil, and the region that has become known as "America's Premier Cultural Resort" boasts the presence of Jacob's Pillow Dance Festival, Shakespeare & Company, and the Berkshire Theater Festival. But the main engine that drives the Berkshires' summertime tourist economy is Tanglewood, the summer residence of the Boston Symphony Orchestra.

I am a total musical rube, devoid of rhythm and tinny of ear. Pretty much everything I know about classical music I learned from repeatedly watching "A Clockwork Orange" in college, and then overhearing restaurant soundtracks while serving sweetbreads and Sancerre. And yet one of the joys I have long associated with the Berkshire food and wine business has been the opportunity to feed some of the world's most accomplished classical musicians, people who turned out to be real human beings in need of food just like everyone else.

I came to accept as my happy responsibility their care and nutrition. After all, they were the primary attraction that drew so many thousands of big-spending visitors during the summer months and therefore made my employment possible. Many of these musicians maintained year-round Berkshire residences, a convenience when performing at Tanglewood but also useful for their weekend getaways throughout the year. It was only natural that I had gotten to know a few of them over the years.

During the summer of 2005 I was still fully involved with my combination gourmet take-out retail store and full-service restaurant. In response to requests from numerous Boston Symphony Orchestra (BSO) musicians, we offered a late-night menu on weekends so that they could eat after their shows. A handful of BSO players from one orchestra section or another showed up every weekend night, just enough to make the late shift worth doing. On one of these Saturday nights, a couple of BSO musicians came by with the Tanglewood Music Center student conductors in tow. They had themselves such a wild time that I regretfully had to send them away in mid-revel at 1:00AM, the legal closing time. In deference to the discriminating ears of my professional musician customers, I refrained from playing background music whenever a quorum of them were present. Conversely, I thought that a slightly obnoxious CD might subtly guide them toward the restaurant's door. This backfired, however, as the group was soon swaying and singing along to the theme from "Shaft," an unlikely candidate for Tanglewood's annual Film Night. The students apparently enjoyed themselves, for they returned the very next night.

Although we weren't offering our late night menu on Sunday evenings after normal business hours, I couldn't bring myself to turn away these new and appreciative customers. I arranged for the three young men to amuse themselves in our otherwise empty dining room with a silky and delicious Pinot Noir from our wine list and some cheeses from our store next door. Once I had them eating and drinking, I couldn't resist asking— "Can you fellas tell me what was up with the cannons at Tanglewood on Parade?" The raucus "1812 Overture," always the concluding piece at Tanglewood's mid-season gala, had been noticeably short on artillery that year.

"You're asking the right person!" chuckled Julian, one of the student conductors. "I was the TMC conductor in charge, and here's what happened…"

Tanglewood's cannoneer, a crusty local fireman, had held the necessary licensure to fire artillery. But thanks to an especially onerous post-9/11 security measure, he had only been able to scrape together enough gunpowder for nine charges instead of the sixteen required in Tchaikovsky's original score. Young Julian had found himself abruptly thrust into the role of a Kissinger-esque diplomat, shuttling between BSO guest conductor Hans Graf and the equally recalcitrant cannoneer until the three of them finally arrived at a compromise. The first volley would be replaced with emphatically loud bass drum, and the second volley would fire as normal. I privately predicted right then that Maestro Julian's knack for such delicate negotiation would surely serve him well as he rose through his professional ranks. Three years later my suspicions were vindicated.

In the summer of 2008, Julian was back in the Berkshires. He had recently been named an assistant conductor for the BSO, a considerable professional accomplishment for someone his age. (He was not yet born when Andrea and I first met.) As we re-acquainted ourselves, he fondly recalled his enjoyable evenings in my restaurant, and we made vague plans to spend a little down time together during his hectic summer.

Over coffee on the Sunday morning after Coach Whalen's mini-camp, I picked Julian's obviously megawatt brain about his job— what, exactly, did a conductor do, and how did he do it? Did he actually make important decisions in real time and instantaneously convey them to his players, like Coach Whalen? A concert attendee, at least one as musically uneducated as I, might rightly wonder whether or not the conductor was absolutely necessary... surely the highly trained musicians must be familiar enough with their parts to play them, no? But I strongly suspected that there was far more to conducting than met my eyes at the few classical concerts I had attended over the years, and Julian patiently gave me a primer.

"It is most important that a conductor understand the composer's original intentions," Julian emphasized, "...understand every decision he made while creating the piece." Of course, there was much, much more to conducting a world-class orchestra than he could explain in one short conversation, much more than I could ever understand. But Julian, who had bravely taken the podium for the ailing BSO director James Levine a few weeks before, was not only a naturally gifted conductor, but also maintained numerous interests beyond music. We eventually found ourselves chatting about rugby, chess, and food and drink. My minimal comprehension of music notwithstanding, Julian's insights would help Andrea and me understand what we were about to witness two days later at Tanglewood on Parade. Five different "big name" conductors were scheduled to perform in fast-paced succession.

To my barely educated eyes that evening, Hans Graf appeared to employ very precise hand movements, obviously doing two very different things with either hand as he guided the BSO through Respighi's "Fountains of Rome." (Maestro Graf had been given very little rehearsal time with the BSO, Julian later explained to me, and had perhaps compensated with precision for what he and the orchestra might have lacked in familiarity.) In contrast, Sir Andrew Davis displayed lots of emotion and expressive body language, conducting the Tanglewood student orchestra with his hair, it seemed, as well as both hands in "Four Sea Interludes" from Britten's opera "Peter Grimes." There appeared to be a high comfort level between Sir Davis and the TMC kids. According to Julian, they had in fact spent many hours together preparing the piece.

Keith Lockhart was up next, conducting the BSO (albeit without its principal players and sitting as the "Boston Pops") in Leonard Bernstein's "Three Dance Episodes" from "On the Town." Unlike any other conductor that night, Maestro Lockhart practically danced through the piece, his hands flashing about like oiled karate. Was that his conducting style, I wondered, or might it have had more to do with composer Bernstein's jazzy music? I suspected that while each conductor has his own personal style, it must also necessarily adapt to the piece at hand.

In stark contrast to Lockhart's mellifluous showmanship, John Williams seemed a rigid, authoritative presence, bringing to my mind a grandfather impatiently marshaling a houseful of young cousins to the washroom before Thanksgiving dinner. But Maestro Williams has always been primarily a TV and movie composer, the father of Hollywood's most recognizable themes. His finale, the familiar "Olympic Fanfare and Theme" on the eve of China's Summer Games, elicited a loud roar of approval from the thousands of picnickers on Tanglewood's vast lawn.

Last up was André Previn, whose smile throughout much of the "1812 Overture" suggested that eighty-year-old men could still have fun doing what they love. Having never before conducted this piece, Maestro Previn seemed to do little more than tap time for the veteran musicians as they navigated this time-worn staple with ease. (As usual, the cannons sounded random and disjointed.)

While watching and comparing these five conductors, my curiosity about them grew. I wanted to learn even more about their extraordinary vocation. Although Julian and I had managed to jointly stage a fun, mid-August dinner party with our ladies— a feast of grilled shrimp and steak, tomato and corn salad, and a Canadian Chardonnay that might well have fooled a native Burgundian— I knew that he was sufficiently busy that I dared not impose further upon his crammed schedule. But I knew another conductor, semi-retired, who might have the time and patience to further school me.

Cellist-conductor Ronald ("Ronny") Feldman retired from the BSO in 2001. He and his harpist wife Elizabeth have since lived in the Berkshires on more of a full-time basis, and had been regular food and wine customers of mine for several years. Like my Andrea, Elizabeth is luminescently beautiful and far younger-looking than her years. One remembers odd little snippets about favorite customers. Of the many unforgettable questions I've fielded from them in my lifetime, this gem of a phone inquiry from Elizabeth about four years before stands out above all others—

"I'm playing with the Beach Boys in Rhode Island this weekend," she began, knowing of my relatively recent fascination with Brian Wilson. "And there's one song in the set that I'm not familiar with. Would you mind singing 'Kokomo' to me?"

Ronny Feldman had joined the Boston Symphony Orchestra as a nineteen-year-old college student in Boston. "I had a low lottery number for the Vietnam war draft," he explained, "so I needed to both stay in school *and* play full-time!" The brilliant student-musician Feldman absorbed enough conducting how-to from his cellist's chair to begin assuming conducting duties himself under John Williams in 1989, and he soon became a regular fixture at the Esplanade podium during Williams' Pops tenure. Upon his retirement from the BSO, Feldman was appointed Artist-in-Residence at Williams College. His duties range from individual music instruction to conducting the *Berkshire* Symphony Orchestra (the "*other* BSO," jokes Feldman), an ensemble comprised of sixty or so accomplished musicians including about two dozen Williams students.

Ronny and Elizabeth invited Andrea and me to join them in their West Stockbridge hillside castle of a home for a late-night dinner of roasted chicken, fresh greens, and a perfectly aged Chianti Classico Riserva that I had actually sold them a few years before. As soon as we arrived, Elizabeth seated us in her spacious practice room and positioned herself in front of one of her four harps, upon which she performed a short welcoming piece for us. It was an upbeat, light dance— a "gavotte," she explained— that had been adapted for harp from early nineteenth-century music. Ronny then led me to his downstairs studio and explained his conducting methodology, occasionally demonstrating with a weightless-looking white baton.

As he begins preparing to conduct a piece, Feldman first addresses what he calls the "blue collar" issues— is everyone playing in tune? Are the three "choirs" (i.e., the strings, the horns, and the winds) in balance? Does everyone share the same understanding of the dynamics (the "louds" and "softs")? As a conductor rehearses with the orchestra, he has already pored over every detail of the score, seeking, like Julian, to understand the composer's original intentions. In doing so, he comes to the rehearsal podium with a very clear opinion as to how the music must be played. It is understood throughout the music world that the conductor's opinion— just like that of a head football coach— is the only opinion that matters.

During his usual quintet of rehearsals before a performance, Maestro Feldman patiently makes all of the corrections he deems necessary, imploring the orchestra to play the piece again and again until they get it right— "so that they can hear it for themselves," as Feldman puts it. Now comes performance night, and all the work has been done, all of the necessary corrections made. Feldman's orchestra knows how the piece should sound, and they are ready to perform it without, as Feldman points out, having lost the important element of spontaneity. As the conductor stands at the podium, baton in hand, he is nominally communicating concrete directions such as "louder" (or "softer") or "faster" (or "slower"). But far more importantly, he is instantaneously communicating with emotion and body language his opinion as to how the piece must sound.

With such valuable inside information from Julian and then Ronny, Andrea and I greatly looked forward to our next Tanglewood concert. However, seats close enough to the stage to actually observe the conducting ("shed seats") were prohibitively expensive. Fortunately for us, I soon learned that feeding hungry musicians had really counted for something. One of the violinists generously treated Andrea and me to what would otherwise have been unaffordable seats, right up front for an all-Mozart program. The performance was Friday, August 8— the date of my sixth chemo infusion.

Sitting directly in front of us that evening were the parents of a young BSO viola player who was engaged to be married immediately after the summer season. Right there during the Mozart concert I arranged to prepare and deliver to their wedding brunch a special smoked salmon platter at a deep discount. Two Fridays later, just hours after my seventh infusion, Andrea and I enjoyed an all-Beethoven program courtesy of the viola player, who sweetly made sure to visually locate us and then discretely wave just before the program began.

"Look at all those fuckin' basses!" I quietly sputtered to Andrea as the players took the stage for Beethoven's Fifth Symphony, the second half of that night's program. We counted ten of the massive stringed instruments, balanced upon their endpins by similarly full-sized men. This famous symphony must require a lot of extra musical horsepower, I figured, but I had never before realized that the instrumental makeup of the orchestra could be adapted so radically from one program to another.

To have heard such a familiar piece played live for the first time was itself amazing; and to have *watched* it and *felt* it performed by one of the world's greatest sitting orchestras and personally knowing so many of the players was even more gratifying. But for so many of these gifted musicians to then smile and wave to us as they left the stage, obviously pleased that Andrea and I were able to attend their concert, delighted my heart and soul beyond measure.

* * * * * * * * *

So went much of our summer of 2008, when we weren't working or keeping my numerous medical appointments... a little football, a little classical music. Coaches and conductors really do have some significant traits in common, I was finally in a position to understand. Maestro Feldman and Coach Whalen share a brilliant, professorial understanding of the arts and sciences that underlie their respective crafts. They have also demonstrated though countless concerts and gridiron victories that they are both accomplished communicators, capable of imparting their accumulated wisdom upon the fortunate Williams students beneath their baton and whistle. I felt proud to know both of these men as I do.

However, just as Maestro Feldman's podium in Chapin Hall and Coach Whalen's domain beside Weston Field are at opposite sides of downtown Williamstown, their very different worlds might well be irreconcilably separated by a vast cultural or even societal gulf. One can no sooner conjure the image of a white bow-tied Coach Whalen bowing deeply to the Williams bleachers after stuffing their archrival Amherst than envision Maestro Feldman's string section jubilantly dousing their conductor with Gatorade after nailing a Mozart requiem.

And yet these two very different worlds can in fact overlap, I discovered just as the summer's waning warmth was giving way to the first gaudy inklings of autumn foliage. On the bright and sunny afternoon of Saturday, September 20, two weeks after my final chemo treatment, I brought Maestro Feldman to a Williams College football game. Coach Whalen warmly welcomed us, first by engulfing me in a congratulatory bear-hug in acknowledgement of my recent negative PET-scan, and then by graciously allowing the two of us sideline privileges so that we could observe up close as he and his assistant coaches called the plays and barked out various commands to their charges.

Shortly after halftime, Williams had the ball near mid-field, third down and a single yard to go. It was a game situation that obviously called for a short yardage running play. Ronny and I watched and listened as Coach Whalen turned to his bench and bellowed in his deliciously deep growl, "MUSCLE! MUSCLE!"

A quartet of towering giants immediately rose and ran out to the Williams huddle, exchanging places with four smaller and quicker-looking players. "Muscle," I concluded, was Whalen's shorthand code for his brawny, short-yardage package, a configuration of his talent pool best suited to the play at hand. I turned to Maestro Feldman and tried to explain it musically as best I could—

"Ronny, I think this is exactly like bringing in all the extra basses for Beethoven's Fifth."

A SEPTEMBER CEASEFIRE

By August's third weekend, my chemo treatments were becoming as thoroughly exhausting and debilitating as Dr. DeLeo had been warning me they would. I was still able to go directly from the chemo salon to Guido's right around the corner and work on Friday afternoons. But chemo Saturdays were becoming more difficult, and chemo Sundays impossible. Meanwhile, the progressively earlier sunsets and nippier night chills were reminders that the summer of 2008 was drawing to a close.

Around mid-August of every year, we Berkshire locals finally become accustomed to summer's relentless gallop. And if our high season were indeed a powerful horse, then we businessmen and laborers who benefit most from summertime trade were the jockeys who must either stay in the saddle or else be thrown and perhaps dragged, boot in stirrup, until Labor Day. As August's dog days slowly scroll we wake up tired, swill coffee, and then hoist ourselves to our cutting boards or retail counters. After double-digit hours on the time clock we indulge in little else but brief, blissful collapse until the next sunrise. When, at last, we reach September's finish line, we dismount and stagger across, thoroughly spent. The Berkshire Summer Season is always a bitch; receiving bi-weekly chemo treatments while working a full schedule made the summer in 2008 far more tiring, much more physically depleting, than had any previous season. By Labor Day I was thoroughly pooped.

But the month of September, I've always been fond of advising customers and friends, is the most beautiful of the Berkshire calendar. The last throngs of summer tourists abruptly vacate the county after Labor Day weekend, relinquishing our roads and cafés to those of us who actually reside here. The September weather, meanwhile, is breathtakingly gorgeous in most years. Increasingly bracing air accompanies sunset as autumn nears, and yet September's days are sunny and warm, generally much less rainy than August's.

Having experienced the excitement of my first Berkshire summer with Andrea— concerts in Tanglewood's shed, salads of locally-grown produce— I had a suggestion for my beloved bride. During the month-long break between my chemo and radiation treatments, we should venture forth upon September's mostly unoccupied roads to explore in detail the small villages that surround the corner where New York, Connecticut, and Massachusetts meet.

On Monday, September first— Labor Day itself— we decided to begin our explorations at the exact locus of this tri-state corner. However, on-line satellite reconnaissance revealed that this point lay deep in heavily forested and mountainous terrain, inaccessible by any road. The nearest trappings of civilization, our laptop maps suggested, was the hamlet of Boston Corner. As viewed in an atlas, this unremarkable stretch of farmland offered little to indicate that one hundred and fifty years ago its mere thousand acres was a notorious refuge for outlaws. It was also the site of a championship boxing match, an event that ultimately prompted an historic secession of territory from one American state to another.

On the map, the lower left corner of Berkshire County appears to have been dog-eared, like the page of a book. Massachusetts originally came to a sharp point at its southwestern-most reach. But this original configuration left the triangle of acreage southwest of the Taconic mountain range beyond the convenient reach of Berkshire County lawmen. Nineteenth-century Boston Corner was accordingly attractive to criminals, gamblers, and other shady types, as they could ply their nefarious trades there relatively unfettered.

Prizefighting had been widely banned during the mid-1800's. Boston Corner, conveniently accessible to Manhattan sports fans via the newly-built Harlem Valley Railroad Line and yet without effective local law enforcement, was thus a logical venue for an illicit, big-purse title fight in 1853. But when thousands of visiting fans rioted and pillaged the nearby farms after the 37-round bout's controversial decision, Massachusetts and New York authorities finally recognized that a reconfiguration of their border was in order. The justifiably enraged citizenry of Boston Corner, having previously petitioned the Commonwealth of Massachusetts to be annexed to New York five years earlier, finally got their wish. The United States Congress approved the change in January of 1855, effective two years hence.

The sudden proximity of policemen and judges succeeded in driving the more colorful elements from Boston Corner. John Morrissey, the young winner of the infamous fight, went on to amass a gambling fortune and eventually partnered with William Travers and others to establish the Saratoga Race Course. After maneuvering his way with his wits as well as his fists into the favor of Tammany Hall, Morrissey was elected to the United States House of Representatives in 1866 and served two terms. Our Labor Day exploration of Boston Corner's few roads and tranquil pastures eventually brought us to a cornfield's official historical marker— albeit with an incorrect date given for the bout— that seemed to be the only remaining physical evidence of either Morrissey's victory or Boston Corner's ribald past.

Our road trip continued south from Boston Corner to nearby Millerton, New York, another village along the now-abandoned northernmost stretch of the Harlem Line. Millerton's old train station, a typical study in rural railroad architecture with ornate wooden brackets supporting its generous eaves, stood empty. However, real estate signs in its windows suggested that it would soon be reborn, perhaps as a restaurant or some sort of store.

There appeared to be several "new Millerton" businesses similarly occupying "old Millerton" property. The Movie House offered independent and lesser-known films in a former grange hall, and right next door the Irving Farm Coffee House, open only since 2003, served its locally-roasted gourmet brew in an obviously time-worn space. A hip little restaurant, Manna Dew, seemed geared more toward homesick and hungry New Yorkers than to the natives. Newly sprouted galleries and boutiques were interspersed with an old-school department store and a bait-and-tackle shop, suggesting that Millerton was becoming a second home for an ever-increasing influx of weekending New Yorkers... a "mini Great Barrington," according to Irving Farm's hardworking proprietor.

From Millerton we traveled south for a few miles and then crossed over into Connecticut. We followed a series of meandering mountain roads out of precious little downtown Kent into Litchfield. As in many of the towns in Berkshire County, Litchfield's swank restaurants and stores seemed uniformly geared toward wealthy weekend and summer visitors, much farther along in this particular evolution than Millerton. It was clearly the summer season's end in Litchfield, for our stroll around town followed mostly empty sidewalks.

Route 63 guided us back toward Great Barrington that afternoon. As we drove, September's sky was a couple of shades bluer than August's, the sultry late-summer air more fragrant yet with scents of the harvest. Corn season was over, but roadside farmstands were a-burst with ruby-ripe tomatoes and perfumed by bunches of deep emerald basil suitable for making gutsy, garlicky pesto. As dusk neared I felt electrified, as always, by the first delicious hints of autumn— the dashes of rust in the Kelly-green Litchfield Hills, the crackling evening air. This was fortuitous timing, because I would need all the energy I could muster to make it through the following weekend.

* * * * * * * * *

My eighth and final appointment with Nurse Elaine— by now, jokingly, my "other woman" according to Andrea— fell on Friday, September 5. With this last chemo infusion, I would be way more than halfway to being completely cured, I naïvely estimated. The chemo was surely the hard part, and in comparison the upcoming radiation should be a bloodless, needle-less cakewalk. Because I had never felt any actual physical symptoms of Hodgkin Lymphoma other than the lump that Dr. Namon had removed, I actually couldn't tell whether or not I was getting healthier. But if the side effects of my chemotherapy were a penance-like indication, I was indeed well on my way to being saved from cancer by treatments whose underlying science I now mostly understood and even more completely trusted.

Andrea and I had welcomed my mother to Berkshire Hematology & Oncology's infusion room so she could finally observe firsthand one of my chemotherapy sessions. We wanted to convincingly demonstrate to her that cancer was not necessarily terminal, and that its treatment could actually be a positive, cheerful experience. A short while later June B. unwittingly reinforced our intentions when she appeared with her oldest daughter to blow celebratory bubbles and thereby mark the end of my chemotherapy. With BHO's wireless Internet service I was able to download a recording of Sir Edward Elgar's "Pomp and Circumstance March #1" from the "Clockwork Orange" soundtrack and play it on my laptop for Elaine as she injected me with the last of my chemo drugs. We were joined in my "graduation march" by a few of the other nurses and even neighboring patients, one of whom had "coded" just a few minutes earlier.

As I might well have expected, this last infusion affected me the hardest, like the final punch in a boxer's flurry that temporarily sends his opponent to dreamland. As I shuffled toward Andrea's car that Friday afternoon there was no enlivening steroid buzz... had Elaine forgotten it? Immediately upon returning to our apartment I collapsed as if boneless into our thick bedding. I was physically unable to keep our tentative dinner appointment that evening with June B., barely capable, even, of rising to use the bathroom.

After my final Sunday morning Neulasta shot and a quick stop at Guido's, I suggested to Andrea that I felt just energetic enough for a brief nature stroll. Surely a little exercise would hasten my recovery from this deepest of chemo stupors, I foolish enough to believe.

High up in the nearby Taconic Mountain Range, Bash Bish Brook careens in a manner akin to its name between the piney slopes overlooking Boston Corner. Its roaring, sixty-foot plunge into a crystalline mountain pool, the Bay State's highest waterfall, is accessible to hikers in Bash Bish Falls State Park as well as from New York's adjoining Taconic State Park. The short trek from the Massachusetts-side parking area to the falls looked easy on the map, especially if one fails to consider, as we had, its precipitously steep descent and the necessary return climb to one's vehicle.

Exhausted as I was, we were motivated apace along the treacherously rocky trail by tree-mounted posters warning of rattlesnakes in the vicinity. And though the stairway to our third-floor apartment felt like a comically cruel continuation of the unexpectedly tough hike, our tranquil half-hour upon the sunny boulders beneath the falls had been well worth the effort to reach them. I again fell into bed and unconsciousness came almost immediately, with my alarm set for 6:00AM on Monday morning so that I could keep yet another chemo-weekend promise.

Given September's sapphire skies and relatively underutilized food service infrastructure, I have always wondered why more couples didn't schedule their Berkshire weddings accordingly. Mr. and Mrs. Siegel of Toronto had wisely planned their daughter Meredith's nuptials for the weekend after Labor Day. Aside from the advantages of perfect weather and empty hostelries, an early September wedding was necessitated by Meredith's work schedule— she was the young BSO violist whose parents had sat in front of us for the all-Mozart program and planned the Monday morning wedding brunch with us.

Mondays were always the hardest days of my chemo hangovers, and of course Monday, September 7 was the worst. But I have always been able to rely upon my adrenaline for accomplishing important tasks such as that before me that morning. From the supplies I had purchased from Guido's after my final Sunday Neulasta shot, I arranged fancy smoked salmon platters garnished with slices of tomato and red onion. Andrea and I provided the ingredients at wholesale cost, and also personally donated a few extra goodies— a homemade spread of cream cheese luxuriously laced with chévre and fresh herbs, and a bottle of "Eroica" Riesling, named for Meredith's favorite Beethoven symphony.

A week after Meredith's wedding brunch, I drove Andrea to yet another nearby village in order to show her one more important piece of my past.

While the village Millerton, New York might well be turning into a "mini Great Barrington," the town Great Barrington in turn had evolved in less than a decade from a row of shuttered businesses into a clone of Northampton, Massachusetts. Once a dowdy and run-down village itself, "Noho" had been reborn and now bustled with pricy shops, nightlife, and of course coffee shops. I alerted Andrea that although Great Barrington was blessed with its generous share of circle-chanting New-Agers, the Northampton area made our Berkshires seem by comparison like a right-wing Christian compound. Taken as a whole, I explained, Northampton was a vibrant blend of the fun, the flaky, and the finer things in life… a great place to spend (or perhaps prolong) one's early adulthood.

My later years of college in the early 1980's coincided with the final stages of downtown Northampton's renaissance. Lucrative restaurant employment was easy to find in such a setting, and I served fancy, expensive dinners in trendy restaurants all over town. After midnight I often roamed Northampton's empty streets and alleys, from the east-side railroad tracks across town to the park-like Smith College campus. With a little imagination and wine, this sometimes felt a little like a mounted nobleman patrolling his sleeping fiefdom. On warm nights I occasionally relaxed in the solitude of the wee hours among the giant sculptures in Smith's art museum courtyard, and a few times I even showed a curious Smith student how to sneak into her college's exotic tropical greenhouse for an illicit midnight picnic beneath its palms.

In contrast to the untamed mountain brook slashing its way through Bash Bish Falls State Park, the manicured campus of Smith College was gently bisected by the not-so-mighty Mill River. The steam shovel had long ago imposed upon it a picturesque waterfall and pond, complete with a cute little island. The deck of Smith's timeworn boathouse stood at this man-made pond's edge— close enough, in winter, to skate directly on to the ice; and, in the warmer months, to step unexpectedly into the dark drink in one's formalwear amidst a romantic, after-party stroll.

I delighted in retracing my old paths with Andrea, showing her by that night's especially bright moonlight Smith's ancient bench swing, the waterfall, and the Japanese tea hut in the woods beside the pond… all, miraculously, while avoiding any self-incrimination as to how I had become so intimately familiar with the all-female college's real estate. Whether it was the exercise or my R-rated recollections (counterbalanced, in my conscience, by memories of young Andrea's scores of male admirers), our walk enlivened me instead of draining my remaining energy.

Two days later we were back on another steep wilderness trail in the Berkshires. Monument Mountain looms seven hundred feet above the Great Barrington high school of the same name. Though it isn't really much of a mountain (it is formally known as "Squaw Peak") most of Monument Mountain is sheer cliff, making the climb to the top relatively short and stair-like. Even experienced and healthy hikers occasionally stop to reclaim their breath. Like nearby Bash Bish Falls, Monument Mountain has long attracted nature-loving Berkshire visitors. Around the same time as the infamous Boston Corner title fight, locally-connected New England authors Nathaniel Hawthorne and Herman Melville were reportedly climbing this little mountain together when a sudden thunderstorm forced to them into a cave, where they allegedly hashed out ideas for Melville's Moby Dick while waiting out the rain.

Monument Mountain's rocky summit was treeless as if above the timberline. As such, it was especially conducive to contemplating its long vistas and the gracefully circling birds of prey while we sunned in silence on the warm and cloudless September afternoon. The only audible evidence of civilization was the distant din of the high school's marching band as they rehearsed for Saturday's football game. The late summer warmth notwithstanding, football season had begun. As Andrea and I navigated the return trail to my car, Coach Whalen's Williams College football players were simultaneously jogging out to their practice field in preparation for their season-opening game three days later against Colby College.

Maestro Ronny Feldman and I absorbed face-on the unimpeded September sun while standing on the Williams sideline that Saturday afternoon. The day itself seemed unable to decide whether it was summer or autumn… pure blue sky, still of wind; dry, and blindingly bright; and yet just short of uncomfortably warm. Such ambiguous weather was fitting— the autumnal equinox, the exact division between seasons, fell just two days hence.

* * * * * * * * *

Raphael Vineyard & Winery on the north fork of Long Island usually harvests its first grapes of the vintage right around the autumnal equinox. Although its sixty acres of vines yield predominantly red wine grapes, five were planted to early-ripening Sauvignon Blanc, in the tradition of the great Bordeaux estates upon which Raphael was modeled. Raphael's winemaker and managing director Richard Olsen-Harbich had decided that Wednesday, September 24th was the best day for their harvest, and without any prior planning whatsoever we jumped at the chance to join him for the occasion.

Long Island's East End might have seemed a world away from our Berkshires, but a giant ferry boat offered a significant shortcut across Long Island Sound as well as a welcome break from highway driving. Separated from the Connecticut shore by only a few miles of water, outermost Long Island might well be considered part of New England. It was settled by the same stock of colonists, who named many of their new towns (e.g., Southold and Easthampton) after their English homelands. In fact, almost everything about East End, from its architecture to its geology, is identical to southern New England's. Long Island, however, was much more generously blessed by nature for wine cultivation.

Even through my chemotherapy treatments I had enjoyed sharing with Andrea my knowledge of wine and the factors that determined its quality— grape variety, winemaking technique, and, most importantly, the growing climate. We had recently driven an hour south from Great Barrington to visit Connecticut's Hopkins Vineyard, the winery I believe to be New England's finest. On our trip across Long Island Sound's choppy blue waters, I explained to Andrea how our destination that afternoon had become one of the world's newest high-quality wine-producing regions.

In the early 1970's, a young couple fresh out of Harvard undertook a nationwide search for vineyard land suited to replicating the French wines they had shared in Cambridge. They eventually settled upon Long Island's north fork, an agricultural Eden blessed with relentless sunshine and an especially long, Bordeaux-like growing season. Alex and Louisa Hargrave

128

harvested their first grapes in 1976 from the vines they had planted, with equal parts optimism and naïveté, in a former Cutchogue potato field. Soon other intrepid winemakers joined them, and by the early 1980's a regional industry had been established. Raphael Vineyard & Winery, founded in 1996, was among the newest, built upon the hard-earned experience of local veterans such as winemaker Richard Olsen-Harbich.

During his long and successful career of Long Island winemaking, Olsen-Harbich (along with a handful of others) had successfully demonstrated that Long Island's climate and soil could fully ripen many of the world's most important grape varieties. With proper and accordingly expensive equipment such as virgin French oak barrels ("new wood," in the winemaking parlance with which I had been familiarizing Andrea) skilled hands such as Olsen-Harbich's had regularly crafted Long Island grapes into excellent wines. His 1988 Bridgehampton Winery "Grand Vineyard" Chardonnay had been the first and only wine from the nascent region to make Wine Spectator magazine's annual "Top 100" list.

I had gotten to know the Long Island wine region in general and Richard Olsen-Harbich in particular when I had operated a wine distribution business in addition to my restaurant endeavors. While distributing Raphael's wines in Massachusetts, Richard and I had become quite brotherly, and my unannounced appearance with Andrea to assist in his first harvest of 2008 seemed like a very pleasant surprise to him. Richard assigned Andrea the task of removing leaves from the grapes on the conveyor belt as they traveled toward the stainless steel winemaking equipment, affording her the opportunity to secretly chant the *Gayathri* mantra over his freshly picked crop. Meanwhile, I operated the screw pump that sent the de-stemmed fruit through heavy piping across the cellar floor to the basket press. As in Septembers past, Raphael's entire 2008 crop of Sauvignon Blanc made the journey from vine to fermenting tank in just a few hours.

I had previously informed Richard of my cancer, and of my marriage to Andrea. Although he seemed relieved to see me still alive and smiling, he was clearly heart-struck by the physical consequences of my treatments evident in my hairless head and putty-like complexion. As we toiled,

Andrea caught him occasionally gazing upon me with an expression suggesting deep concern.

Richard and I had long shared all manner of locker room dialogue in addition to thoughts on wine. Sensing this, and perhaps hoping to reassure Richard of my favorable prognosis, Andrea obliquely suggested that our chemo-impaired sex life had recently returned perforce to normalcy. "Talk about NEW WOOD!" she mischievously gushed to Richard.

"You two are PERFECT for each other!" he heartily proclaimed, shaking his head with laughter. He could tell that we were very happy together, and that Andrea was making my battle with cancer much more bearable. In a few hours we were on the road back toward home, with Richard's 2008 Sauvignon Blanc safely in his fermenting tank and a mixed case of Raphael wines in our trunk, a generous wedding gift. We would be back the following summer, we promised, to purchase a case of the wine that we had personally seen created.

* * * * * * * *

Although it was well after our wedding, and we had never strayed very far from our tiny Great Barrington apartment, our September road trips during the pause in my treatment had actually felt like a honeymoon. Perhaps because of my cancer it was with heightened awareness, a newfound appreciation for the joys of nature within reach of our Great Barrington home, that Andrea and I had so thoroughly enjoyed the month of September. Soon my ceasefire would be over, and I would be back to war... nuclear war, actually, as my introductory appointment at Berkshire Medical Center's Radiation Oncology department was scheduled right at the end of September.

$$E = mc^2$$

Having endured my eight "innings" of chemotherapy treatments— better, I naturally hoped, than had my cancer cells— it was now time to finish off what might be left of them with radiation therapy. In other words, my body was about to be bombarded with something that I had been conditioned nearly from birth to regard as deadly and frightening. As usual, this inspired me to obsessively research the topic. It also gave me cause to reflect upon my lifelong acquaintance with radiation in its various forms.

* * * * * * * * *

As a tail-end baby boomer born near the end of the Eisenhower presidency, such terminology as "radiation" and "nuclear" automatically conjures in my mind vivid imagery of glowing atomic explosions. Graduating from Berkshire Hematology & Oncology's chemo salon to the radiation oncology department at Berkshire Medical Center on the other side of Pittsfield inspired a different sort of flashback, back to my high school days. In a sense, it was like crossing Wayne Central's science hallway from the eleventh-grade chemistry lab to the senior class physics room. (Beautiful young Andrea's locker was way on the other side of the sprawling, one-story building.) But much earlier in my schooling, long before my high school years or any amorous thoughts of my eventual wife, I had become vaguely aware of this strange, invisible thing called radioactivity.

I entered primary school in the early 1960's. I still clearly recall our first-grade "duck-and-cover drills" in which we were taught to dive beneath our gum-barnacled classroom desks in preparation for the half-expected nuclear attack by the communists... which, of course, would have rendered us indistinguishable from all that gum no matter where we had sought cover. While my six-year-old brain had lacked the capacity to comprehend the particulars of the relevant science, this Cold War introduction to its potential ramifications had stamped upon my brow a permanent fascination with the subject.

Electromagnetic radiation, I was surprised to learn in my high school physics class, was absolutely everywhere around us. In order of increasing energy, it emanated from radio towers, microwave ovens, baseboard heaters, tanning booths, and our family dentist's x-ray machine. And it has always been present among us, even before these inventions. Sunshine itself has bombarded Earth with these very same wavelengths since the creation of our solar system. Furthermore, the range of radiation between the baseboard warmth (infrared) and the tanning rays (ultraviolet) constitutes the spectrum of visible light, from the crimson autumn foliage to the cornflower blue in the September sky.

It suddenly seemed to my twelfth-grade brain as if most everything around me was radiation of one form or another, and that seemingly solid objects were of ambiguous composition, given the nature of basic matter at the sub-atomic level. Interestingly, mankind's understanding of electromagnetic radiation was barely over a century old. Investigation into the sub-atomic universe was a relatively recent advance in a progression of scientific inquiry that had begun during the renaissance.

Galileo Galilei bequeathed to mankind his groundbreaking and useful theories of gravitation and motion. Building largely upon Galileo's foundation, Sir Isaac Newton (1643-1727) constructed his famous laws of motion involving "equal and opposite reactions" and such. All manner of physical phenomena, from planetary motion to the workings of the steam engine, were explainable by "classical Newtonian mechanics," the derivative offspring of Newton's laws.

However, discoveries in the fields of electricity and magnetism during the second half of the nineteenth century began to raise questions that no existing scientific theory could answer. Particles moving at velocities approaching the speed of light, for example, exhibited unexpected physical changes as well as wave-like characteristics. But then the Scottish mathematician and physicist James Clerk Maxwell (1831-1879) succeeded in developing a consistent theory that explained the interwoven relationships among electricity, magnetism, and light. This resulted in a breathtakingly swift scientific boom.

As if a dam had suddenly burst, there ensued during the seven-and-a-half decades extending from the end of the American Civil War to the first shots of World War II a non-stop barrage of discovery without equal in human history. The roster of contributing scientists reads like the scoreboard of a European chess tournament:

Röntgen of Prussia— x-rays;

Becquerel of France— natural radioactivity in uranium ore;

The Curies of Poland and France— discovery of radioactive elements;

Einstein of Germany— relativity and mass-energy equivalence;

Bohr of Denmark— the atomic model;

Enrico Fermi of Italy— nuclear fission and chain reactions.

By the time war clouds began to darken Europe in the late 1930's, nuclear physicists understood that tiny amounts of matter could be converted into vast amounts of pure energy in the form of radiation. This had potential applications in electrical power generation, medicine... and, for better or worse, warfare. As World War II loomed, this was a terrifying prospect.

Many of the European physicists were of Jewish descent, and had fled the continent as Hitler amassed power. Fearful that the Third Reich might be advancing toward nuclear weaponry, they encouraged Einstein, by far the most influential among them, to write to President Roosevelt encouraging American nuclear development. *"...Extremely powerful bombs of a new type may thus be constructed,"* warned Einstein in a 1939 letter. The resulting American effort was code-named the "Manhattan Project."

The production of atomic energy via nuclear fission entails splitting a heavy atom, such as Uranium-235 or Plutonium-239, by striking it with a neutron— kind of like splitting a massive ash log with a comparatively tiny wedge. The original atom is transformed into two smaller atoms while releasing additional neutrons, which go on to split neighboring atoms in a continuous chain reaction. (How the axe-man would appreciate a similar effect at his woodpile!)

The mass of the components resulting from these repeated atomic divisions is less than that prior to the collisions. The difference, though miniscule, is converted into an enormous amount of high-energy electromagnetic radiation in accordance with Einstein's famous equation. Here nuclear energy derived from fission takes two distinct forms— a slow rate of reaction that generates the steady flow of heat useful for peaceful electrical production, and a lightning-quick reaction that yields a militarily useful detonation.

A far more powerful nuclear *fusion* bomb, in which two small atoms (hydrogen isotopes) would be "fused" into a larger (helium) atom, was a possibility considered by the Manhattan Project physicists. This is precisely how our sun works. Such a "thermonuclear" weapon would be many times more powerful than a fission device, and generate energies previously unthinkable on planet Earth. But a fusion bomb would have required an initial *fission* detonation in order to set it off, and so they focused instead on the development of the simpler bomb, as their immediate goal of attaining nuclear capability before the Axis powers was deemed to be quite time-sensitive.

As soon as World War II ended, most of the globe immediately realigned into opposing political-ideological camps— the Soviet bloc, and the "free world." The United States, weary of warfare and yet suddenly facing a new world order and a new set of enemies, embarked on the rapid expansion of her nuclear arsenal. The Soviets were able to do the same, having shrewdly positioned several spies within the Manhattan Project. The nuclear fusion weapon, also known as the "hydrogen bomb" (or the "H-bomb," for short) was ready for use by both sides merely seven years after Japan's surrender… and thus became synonymous with the horrifying specter of a thermonuclear World War III.

Dwight D. Eisenhower, America's most respected war general, took the oath for the presidency in 1953. He wasted no time in framing his geo-political world view, observing in his inaugural address that *"Forces of good and evil are massed and armed and opposed as rarely before in history... freedom is pitted against slavery; lightness against the dark."* Winning this ideological and perhaps military battle, Eisenhower strongly believed, would require lots of nuclear bombs as well as the means to deliver them, either as a convincing deterrent or an actual military option. In contrast to a huge standing army and conventional munitions, nuclear weaponry was considerably more cost-effective— more "bang for the buck," as Ike was fond of saying.

During the first year of Eisenhower's grandfatherly, two-term watch, he attempted to paint a more benevolent countenance on America's nuclear might with his "Atoms for Peace" United Nations speech. In it, he proposed the development of nuclear power plants around the globe— thus inadvertently hastening, maybe, the proliferation of nuclear arms among countries such as Pakistan and India. Meanwhile, Ike maintained a clenched fist behind his extended olive branch as he oversaw America's deployment of the nuclear-armed B-52 Flying Stratofortress, perpetually airborne worldwide; nuclear-powered submarines on constant patrol and loaded with Polaris nuclear missles; and the development of land-based intercontinental ballistic missiles (ICBM's) capable of reaching Moscow from their underground silos in America's heartland. (*"Guaranteed worldwide delivery in thirty minutes or less..."* according to chilling graffiti supposedly discovered in one of the silo's stairwells after the Cold War, *"...or the next one's FREE!"*)

Even our present Interstate highway system was part of Eisenhower's nuclear program. It was originally designed to facilitate emergency aircraft landings as well as the orderly evacuation from metropolitan areas under attack, complete with its exit curves sufficiently banked to prevent the famously top-heavy Jeep from overturning. Amazingly, Eisenhower managed to accomplish all of this without running up a federal deficit— unlike President Reagan and his military-industrial minions, who eventually *outspent* the Soviets into submission.

In retrospect, General Eisenhower might well be remembered as our nuclear President, one whose belief in the black-and-white moral superiority of American-style freedom over Soviet totalitarianism come war or not might now seem quaint to many. Was he wrong? Or perhaps overly simplistic? Given the times and the known record of America's

Cold War adversary, I don't think so. The post-war Soviet Union was a snarling, menacing bear that had devoured several of her small neighboring countries without compunction. Might Western Europe have been on their menu as well? "All the Soviets required to reach the English Channel," observed the American Under Secretary of State Robert A. Lovett after the Stalin-backed Czech coup of 1948, "was shoes."

Furthermore, history teaches us that Russian rulers, communist or otherwise, have long placed as little significance in body counts as in the international treaties to which they have affixed their signatures. After all, there was always plenty of vacant real estate for burying their war dead, and no free press to report their numbers. Indeed, the Russian concept of military victory has sometimes seemed at odds with its generally accepted definition. Consider, for instance, Tchaikovsky's "1812 Overture," the annual finale piece at Tanglewood On Parade as well as a summertime staple of outdoor orchestras across the country. Over the past few decades, the bombastic "1812" has become oddly associated with America's annual Fourth of July celebration, right alongside our most cherished patriotic hymns. Lost in the excitement of the fireworks and munitions, however, is the minor detail that the "1812 Overture" was originally composed to celebrate the seventieth anniversary of Russia's "triumph" over the invading armies of France.

Some triumph, an objective historian might harrumph. The glorious victory celebrated in Tchaikovsky's most recognizable opus transpired only because the Russians had torched Moscow, their once and future capital, to the ground, thereby hastening the wintertime retreat to Poland by Napoleon's decimated and starving troops. One hundred and thirty years later, when the U.S.S.R. had nominally been our ally in World War II, her share of Germany's defeat had come at a cost of over ten million Soviet corpses— a full forty percent of the war's total military toll. In retrospect, therefore, it seems plausible that the Soviets might have willingly absorbed an incoming American H-bomb or two during the Cold War in order to achieve their long-term goals.

However, the Soviets had perhaps considered America's overwhelming air, land, and sea-based nuclear supremacy with an especially sober eye and saw certain suicide in any excessively aggressive behavior... if not "mutually assured destruction," then surely their own. By matching the Soviets nuke-for-nuke and then some, President Eisenhower might well have saved the world from thermonuclear war during and long after his presidency. As such, America's Cold War nuclear capability might well have been, ironically, the single greatest instrument of *peace* in the history of mankind.

But peaceful nuclear power is another story.

As if my first-grade experience with air-raid drills hadn't left enough of a nuclear impression upon my young mind, the following summer my father moved us to Ontario, New York. There, on Lake Ontario's southern shore, a nuclear power plant was under construction. Rochester Gas & Electric, the plant's original corporate owner, had set a thorough public relations scheme in place. Year after year my Wayne Central science teachers extolled the many environmental *benefits* afforded by this facility. It didn't hurt RG&E's position within Wayne Central's halls that they were by far the single biggest property-tax payer into our tiny school district's coffers. Even so, the word "radiation" was tossed about from time to time with a hint of trepidation.

I was in college when the Three Mile Island disaster eerily coincided with Hollywood's release of "The China Syndrome," raising concerns about nuclear power plant safety that would never completely go away. One spring semester I had the unexpected honor of studying statistics under a science professor who had worked on the first such facilities in the 1950's. "You have to understand," he apologetically explained to the class, "we thought we were saving the world... providing impoverished countries with electrical power that was literally *too cheap to meter.*" We forgave him, I sensed.

But nuclear power had turned out to be far more expensive than he had imagined possible, for he and his fellow generation of nuclear engineers had failed to consider the costs of safely storing nuclear waste for many thousands of years. They had neglected to do so because they had assumed that the production of electricity by nuclear fission— with its attendant hazardous waste— was just a temporary measure until fusion could be effectively harnessed. But while the military's progression from fission to fusion had only taken seven years, it eventually became apparent that the transition to peaceful fusion would take far longer. And there was another problem with nuclear energy, I came to believe as I pursued my undergraduate studies in environmental economics.

During my junior year of college I became aware of a second school of thought above and beyond simple cost-benefit analysis. "Buddhist Economics," for lack of a formal description, amounts to "doing the most with the least," thrift and simplicity for its own sake... technology appropriate to the task. The authors we revered, E. F. Schumacher and his ilk, decried the nuclear generation of electricity as environmental and technological overkill... "cutting butter with a chainsaw," as we delighted in disparaging it.

And here America was, vigorously pursuing the development of fusion power, as if it was the magic solution to every imaginable scarcity. If splitting atoms to boil water was akin to cutting butter with a chainsaw, then essentially forming an artificial sun to accomplish the same task was self-evidently ridiculous, we thought. Why split an atom with a neutron when splitting a log with an axe would accomplish the same thing? Why ignite another sun instead of a wood stove? A few years after my college graduation, the Chernobyl disaster of 1986 underscored the high risk fundamentally inherent in such overly centralized technology.

But to be fair, there is something to be said for the advance of technology for its own sake, too. Just as America's space program yielded a number of completely unexpected benefits ranging from cordless power tools to telecommunications, advances in nuclear science, both military and peaceful, have long cross-pollinated each other. For better or worse, twentieth century science had successfully harnessed the forces of the inner atom to many different uses— military, peaceful... and medical. Which brings us back to radiological medicine, the third major application of twentieth-century nuclear physics after warfare and power generation—

I was about to have my cancerous tumors bombarded with the very same sort of radiation from which I once practiced hiding beneath my first-grade desk.

The notion of striking out the remainder of my cancer with something that I had been conditioned nearly from birth to regard as deadly and frightening took more effort to absorb, actually, than would the radiation itself. While researching the medical use of radiation, I promptly found confirmation of my well-learned fears— the very same high-energy electromagnetic radiation that I would be receiving was indeed considered toxic. In February of 2005, the U.S. Department of Health and Human Services added x-rays and gamma rays to its list of consumable goods and environmental components that are either known to cause or can be "reasonably anticipated" to cause cancer. In the case of radiation, this means thyroid, breast, and lung cancers, as well as leukemia. Of course, we had already seen vivid proof of this in Japan in the aftermath of World War II.

* * * * * * * * *

Dr. Michael DeLeo had been my starting pitcher, the wizardly Ace who had successfully mixed his four different pitches to hurl eight scoreless innings. The score, according to my PET-scan at the conclusion of my chemotherapy, was in our favor— I was officially in remission. But we couldn't stop there. In baseball, a team behind by many runs still gets its chance to bat in the ninth. Likewise, with Hodgkin Lymphoma, the established "standard of care" called for radiation after the chemotherapy. So now it was time to call the bullpen and summon a specialist to finish the job, to chalk up the three final outs… not with fastballs, but rather with photons of electromagnetic radiation.

It was time to bring in The Closer.

THE CLOSER

Major League Baseball is big business; serious money is at stake on the outcome of every game. This is why every club strives to keep on its pitching staff one special reliever whose assignment is simplicity itself— preserve his team's narrow advantage by overpowering and shutting down the opposition's best hitters in the ninth and final inning. This pitcher is known as The Closer.

Starting pitchers by necessity bring a variety of pitches to the mound, but The Closer usually relies upon his single most formidable delivery, typically a blazing fastball or one of its sinking, slicing variants. And while the starter has numerous innings over which to spread his occasional human failings, The Closer enjoys no such margin for error. A solitary lapse in the ninth inning can instantly turn victory into defeat.

By the nature of his high-profile and pressure-packed role, The Closer often stands well apart from his fellow major-leaguers. He tends to carry himself like a larger-than-life loner, a cross-breed, perhaps, of an Old West cowboy and a flamboyant professional wrestler. As such, he seems to bristle with palpable intensity and even an air of dangerousness.

* * * * * * * * *

The Hall of Fame relief pitcher Roland Glen "Rollie" Fingers of my beloved 1970's Oakland A's teams remains my favorite baseball player of all time. Fingers was so reliably dominant in the late innings, so elemental to the A's' trio of World Series titles, that he unwittingly pioneered the role of "Closer" during his long and successful career. His was a commanding presence. On a colorful pitching staff armed by such men as Jim "Catfish" Hunter and John "Blue Moon" Odom, Rollie Fingers needed no nickname. And on a team paid bonuses by its maverick owner to grow mustaches, Fingers' Gilded-Age handlebar brought to mind an icewater-veined gunslinger at high noon as time and time again he calmly took the mound and finalized a slim lead.

Thanks in large part to Fingers' example, Cooperstown has reserved space beside him for a handful of his fellow Closers... each with his own signature pitch, almost like a professional wrestler's "patented finishing hold."

During a relief career that endured until his age nearly equaled his deceptively feeble pitching velocity, Hall-of-Famer Hoyt Wilhelm bedeviled a whole generation of late-inning batters with his maddeningly fluttering knuckleball. His fellow inductee Richard "Goose" Gossage, on the other hand, was a more typical Closer, an unreconstructed flamethrower who regularly broke the 100 MPH barrier. Bruce Sutter merited enshrinement for likewise finishing off hundreds of opponents with his sinking, split-fingered fastball. The current Yankee Closer (and future Hall of Fame lock) Mauriano "Mo" Rivera is synonymous with his wickedly breaking "cutter," a fastball sub-type so troublesome that it occasionally prompts switch-hitters to change sides and bat righty-against-righty rather than shatter their bats.

In another noteworthy similarity to professional wrestling, some marquee Closers have taken to dramatically entering games accompanied by their personal "theme music." The all-time leading career Closer Trevor Hoffman will be long remembered for his Wrestlemania-like entrance into home games, theatrically strolling in from the bullpen to the creepy strains of AC-DC's "Hell's Bells." Mo Rivera, meanwhile, regularly ascends the Yankee Stadium mound to Metallica's "Enter Sandman," an entrance fanfare he shares with mixed martial artist (and former pro wrestler) Brock Lesnar.

After receiving the eighth and last of my chemo infusions, I was ready for the radiation specialist to authoritatively enter the game and shut down my Hodgkin Lymphoma in the ninth inning with fourteen zaps of radiation, fourteen unanswerable fastballs on the edges of the plate. Like a Closer's hapless victims in the batter's box, my cancerous tumors wouldn't be able to adapt and survive the onslaught of photons even if they knew exactly what was coming. The Closer would just have to do his job, finish what the Ace had so ably begun, and then this game would be over.

* * * * * * * * *

During the last week of September I reported for the first of my pre-radiation appointments at Berkshire Radiological Associates, the radiation clinic at Pittsfield's Berkshire Medical Center. At first glance, the place seemed refreshingly less "medical" in comparison to the chemo salon— no stench of chemicals, no needles, no blood-drawing station. There was a waiting room much like that of any other doctor's office, but there were also some very un-physician-like "doctors" striding about who had earned their professional prefixes not in medicine but in nuclear physics. Everyone there, however, was working under the direction of Dr. Wade Gebara, a medical doctor who also understood the finer points of radioactivity.

As I mentally prepared myself to begin my radiation treatments, I naturally wondered— did this Dr. Gebara bear any of the hallmark traits of a genuine Closer? Any Red Sox fan who has witnessed Boston Closer Jonathan Papelbon's half-deranged, post-victory riverdance can attest that this stripe of pitcher tends to flirt with societal boundaries more closely than does the general population. Might this Dr. Gebara have a spicy history, or some sort of quirk that would confirm his Closer status and thus inspire my trust? If he were an actual relief pitcher, what song might be his entrance music?

Dr. Wade Gebara was no more physically imposing than Dr. DeLeo, or, for that matter, the average man on the street. And yet he had an otherworldly cast in his eyes... was it merely a flash of the shimmering intellect behind them, as with my conductor friends? Or, as I fancifully speculated (and kind of hoped) was it a glimpse into something edgier? It didn't take long to find out.

Dr. Gebara's faint, soothing drawl betrayed his rural Georgia origins. His ancestors had been forced to move there from South Carolina during the Civil War, he told me. That was because they had been abruptly dispossessed of their long-held family acreage during General William Tecumseh Sherman's pyromaniacal march to the sea. So far, so good... a nice and homey background tale from the Land of Cotton. But soon thereafter, as Dr. Gebara excitedly explained, his forefathers boldly robbed a Union pay train of its resources, with which they eventually purchased a new family farm.

As Dr. Gebara's oral autobiography unfolded, his Dixie accent deepened and his eyes glistened with fierce, unabashed pride, as if he had been describing, say, an esteemed great-uncle who had served as a U.S. senator rather than a vengeful band of railroad thieves.

This, from the widely renowned cancer doctor who had designed his own linear accelerator as a brilliant college undergrad? And then opted for medical school almost as a whim just before graduation? This, from the doctor who would be treating ME?

As medical doctors go, this as near to an actual Closer type as one gets. I knew right then that Dr. Gebara was the right man for the job. What might have remained of my cancer wouldn't stand a chance against this guy.

* * * * * * * * *

Radiation causes cancer by disrupting the molecular structure of cell DNA and thus prompting unhealthy mutations. Most paradoxically, it cures cancer in much the same way— when properly directed at tumors, radiation disables cancer cells by damaging their DNA beyond repair, leaving them unable to perpetuate their strain. The important trick in radiotherapy is to aim a powerful enough beam with sufficient precision enough to damagingly irradiate all of the cancer cells while sparing the healthy tissue overlying and surrounding the intended target.

As such, the long and often painful evolution of radiotherapy parallels the development of the firearm and its capacity to direct bullets into and through mammalian flesh.

The invention of gunpowder by the Chinese in the thirteenth century soon led to the development of crude rockets and cannons. The portable long gun first appeared in warfare three centuries later. The earliest such weapon was a shoulder-held miniature cannon of sorts, muzzle-loaded with dirty-burning black powder and a more or less round ball of lead. The accuracy of these early "muskets" beyond point-blank range was highly questionable, but with the nineteenth century came the pointed bullet (1823) and then twisted grooves within the barrel ("rifling") that imparted a stabilizing spiral upon it, like a well-thrown football.

The American Civil War was such a horrific bloodbath precisely because, at mid-nineteenth century, mankind's ability to shoot one another had far out-evolved medical science's capacity for treating the wounded. During the succeeding century, the development of powerful smokeless gunpowder along with advances in barrel metallurgy, optics, and manufacturing techniques made possible a sniper rifle capable of ventilating a cereal box a dozen football fields away.

As the rifle evolved, so did the bullet. The round(ish), Revolutionary War-era musket ball, though somewhat effective against human enemies at close range, had little ability to penetrate through protective barriers or into the flesh of a large game animal. Pure lead bullets, even pointed ones, tended to "mushroom" upon impact, and so hard metal jacketing (as in the Vietnam movie "Full Metal Jacket") was introduced to maintain the bullet's shape and thus improve its penetrating ability. But aside from reliably reaching a distant target, a bullet must both penetrate *and* kill. While the leaden ball might ineffectively splatter against bone, the fully-jacketed round might well pass completely through its quarry without imparting instantly lethal damage, affording enemy combatants time to shoot back and wounded game time to run away.

The ideal bullet combines ballistic stability and structural soundness with the ability to transfer all of its lethal energy deep within its target. Today's top safari enthusiasts and shooting aficionados swear by Nosler® bullets— "*when you care enough to send the very best,*" as sardonically sloganeered by their devotees. This state-of-the-art brand of ammunition boasts such features as a boat-tail shape for superior aerodynamics, a thick base to prevent deformation at extremely high muzzle energies, and a jacket of varying thickness so that it peels back upon itself and thus expands at a rate ideal for quick kills.

Dr. Wade Gebara, however, would be shooting at my tumors not with bullets or baseballs, but rather with high-energy photons— sub-atomic, massless packets of pure energy that emanate from radioactive atoms. The photons themselves wouldn't be killing my cancer cells; rather, the beams would strip away electrons from the molecules of my targeted flesh, as a child blows fuzzy white seeds from a dandelion stem. The electrons, upon inheriting the energy from the photons, then fly smack into the cancerous cells. Much like bullets and baseballs, they impart their energy upon that which stopped them. The goal of my radiotherapy team, therefore, was to direct and control the beam of photons so that the resultant flow of electrons would be destructively absorbed by my cancerous cells without shooting the rest of my flesh to pieces.

Needless to say, this would require some especially Big Science.

* * * * * * * *

The underlying science of cancer radiotherapy is even farther beyond the grasp of the average oncology patient than the biochemistry of chemotherapy. Here is how I explained it to myself—

Photons are miniscule packets of pure energy. While major-league fastballs typically reach 95 miles per hour and rifle bullets half a mile per second, photons travel at the speed of light— 186,000 *miles* per second. All electromagnetic radiation, from radio waves to visible light to x-rays, travels in the form of photons. As extremely small and extremely fast physical entities, photons exhibit characteristics of both waves and particles; that is, they each have a particular wavelength. (Don't be intimidated... theoretical physicists can't really "picture" a photon, either. Just think of them as tiny and vibrating bullets or baseballs for now.) Unlike bullets and baseballs, however, photons have no mass. And yet, as packets of pure energy, they have the ability, just like bullets and baseballs, to inflict damage when directed at a target. Furthermore, all photons have equal mass (zero) and travel at identical speeds, yet some pack more energy than others. The shorter the photon's wavelength, the more frantic its "vibration," so to speak, and thus the higher its level of potentially destructive energy.

The energy absorbed by a catcher's mitt receiving a 95 MPH fastball equals one-half of the baseball's mass (5.12 ounces) times the square of its velocity— that comes to about 87 "foot-pounds," the same amount of energy required for a proud dad to hoist his 87-pound Little League son one foot off the ground in a congratulatory hug. Likewise, a typical deer-hunting rifle issues forth a 180-grain (0.4 ounce) bullet at half a mile per second, delivering 2700 foot-pounds of energy into its unfortunate target... enough to raise that Little League dad's Honda Civic a foot above the ground.

But calculating the energy of photons is more complicated than that of baseballs and bullets, as photons are extremely tiny and have no mass. Physicists therefore measure the energy of a continuous stream of photons, just as we would measure the collective force of a flowing river rather than that of its individual drops. The energy associated with a such a stream of photons is inversely proportional to their wavelength, and therefore the beam of mysterious, short-wavelength rays generated in William Conrad Röntgen's laboratory in 1895 was many times more energetic than the visible light that emanated from Thomas Edison's first incandescent bulb just sixteen years before.

Not long after Röntgen's discovery of the band of electromagnetic radiation that he dubbed "x-rays," exposure to it was found to cause cancer as well as, in some cases, temporarily arrest it. Might this power be domesticated for purely beneficial medical uses? Although the earliest x-ray emitters were known to shrink cancerous lymph nodes, they lacked the power to reach tumors deep in the body... just as a crude, low-powered lead ball might bloody the outer flesh of an angry rhinoceros without reaching its innermost organs and thereby halting its deadly charge. However, the development of an improved cathode tube in the 1920's made possible the propagation of x-ray beams many times more powerful than Röntgen's.

Counter-intuitively, perhaps, the more powerful the beam of photons, the less damage it inflicts upon innocent tissue on the way to its cancerous target. It may be useful here to consider that low-energy infra-red radiation, as from glowing barbecue embers, warms our cheeks precisely because the outermost layer of our skin abruptly halts these rays, absorbing all of their energy as heat. And yet more powerful, shorter wavelength radiation— such as x-rays— readily penetrates the skin and underlying flesh without sensation. For infra-red radiation to penetrate human tissue as deeply, it would have to painfully "cook" its way through, as with a leg of lamb slowly roasted to uniform, medium-rare perfection.

Aided by the latest generation of x-ray-producing cathode tubes during the 1920's and '30's, the Swiss physician Dr. René Gilbert was responsible for two important intermediary steps in the cure of Hodgkin Lymphoma. Dr. Gilbert recognized that this disease progressed through the lymph system in an especially orderly manner. By directing radiation not only at the tumor site ("involved field") but also at the adjacent lymph nodes, or "extended field," he was able to intercept the illness and prolong the lives of his patients. And just as a Major League catcher would surely prefer to absorb the energy of thirty-two fastballs rather than the equal amount in a single gunshot, Dr. Gilbert successfully divided radiation treatments into survivable fractions.

Radiation was strong medicine. Dr. Gilbert understood that exposures sufficient to annihilate tumors in a single treatment were also too powerful for surrounding tissue to withstand. But he correctly reasoned that radiation's impact upon cancerous cells would be cumulatively lethal if administered in smaller, "fractionated" doses over the course of many days. Cancer cells cannot repair themselves when injured as readily as can healthy tissue. With correct calibration, therefore, radiation doses could be just strong enough to slowly kill the tumor while only temporarily wounding its surrounding flesh. By receiving treatments over many days rather than in a single, massive dose, Dr. Gilbert's patients were better able to survive and tolerate the necessary amount of radiation while their cancerous cells nonetheless succumbed to its cumulative effect.

Dr. Gilbert, like doctors before him, was limited by the capability of his cathode ray equipment. Superior though it was to its predecessors, it still wasn't quite powerful enough to penetrate as deeply as needed without causing severe skin reactions and other tissue damage. Although Dr. Gilbert could claim in his 1939 retrospective summary of his cases that his Hodgkin Lymphoma patients had lived twice as long as previously expected, an actual cure via radiation, he admitted, remained beyond his reach.

But if photons were bullets in the war against cancer, the devices for delivering them were steadily improving, just as the crude musket eventually evolved into the deadly accurate sniper rifle. Even before Dr. Gilbert summarized his findings, improvements in radiation technology had led to the development of a new type of radiation generator that was twice as powerful as that which he had used. The first Cobalt-60 radiotherapy machine was put into use in a Canadian hospital in 1937. Armed, finally, with the ability to effectively irradiate tumors anywhere in the body, atomic-age medicine found itself within shooting range of Hodgkin Lymphoma's elusive cure.

Building upon Dr. René Gilbert's earlier work, Dr. Gordon Richards and his young protégé Dr. Mildred Vera Peters used this new Cobalt-60 machine at Toronto General Hospital to treat a great number of HL patients. By caring for patients by day and then meticulously reviewing their cases each night, Dr. Peters was able to make useful correlations between the severity (or stage) of a particular case and the effectiveness of various types of radiation treatments— i.e., involved field vs. extended field radiation, high dose vs. low dose radiation, and total nodal irradiation. By the time her mentor died in 1949, Dr. Peters had accumulated enough data from over one hundred well-documented cases to conclude, in a paper she published a year later, that Hodgkin Lymphoma was in fact curable.

Like many of her fellow scientists past and present, Dr. Peters was initially greeted with disbelief and scorn for brashly drawing such a conclusion... perhaps because it was impossible to say exactly when this noble goal had been attained. Unlike, say, a big-game hunter dropping a charging rhino dead in its tracks or a Closer firing a game-ending fastball past a cagy pinch-hitter, achieving victory over Hodgkin Lymphoma was considerably more arbitrary and nebulous... *what percentage* of patients with *what diagnosed stage*— in remission for *how long*— constituted an acceptable cure rate? Furthermore, while breakthrough discoveries in medical science are often credited to individuals, the actual practice of medicine tends to move forward only by profession-wide consensus. By 1963, however, Dr. Vera Peters' lone voice had become a chorus, most notably joined by Dr. Henry Kaplan, part rival and part kindred spirit in the quest for an HL cure through radiotherapy.

In 1956, Dr. Kaplan had arranged the installation of a newer yet type of radiation device in his clinic at Stanford University. His "linear accelerator" was kind of like a drag strip for charged subatomic particles, a machine that electrostatically impelled them to high energies and then smashed them into a Tungsten plate. This collision produced a photon shower more powerful yet than its Cobalt-60 predecessor. Furthermore, it could be aimed precisely enough for Dr. Kaplan to successfully zap a malignant tumor buried deep within a two-year-old's eye every day for six weeks without injuring his lens or cornea. Soon after this success with his very first linear accelerator patient, Dr. Kaplan began to direct his well-disciplined photons at cancerous lymph nodes. His 1963 summary of Stanford's extensive study of radiotherapy for Hodgkin Lymphoma corroborated Dr. Peters' earlier findings and convinced the remaining skeptics that HL was indeed a curable disease.

Forty-five years later, the technology familiar to Dr. Kaplan hadn't changed all that much. On Monday, October 6, I was scheduled to lie beneath a "Varian® Cliniac 21EX" linear accelerator in its lead-lined room at Berkshire radiological associates and personally receive my first blast of radiation, the first pitch of the ninth inning from Dr. Gebara.

* * * * * * * * *

My research into radiotherapy had succeeded in allaying any lingering reservations I may have had about radioactivity. Perhaps because of my lifelong fascination with the topic, I was actually excited and thrilled to finally be entering into my radiation treatments after a summer of chemotherapy. Radiation… Einstein… $E = mc^2$! Gamma rays from a radioactive nucleus, like bourbon straight out of its bottle! Well, not exactly. Although gamma rays are classically defined as radiation with wavelengths slightly shorter yet than x-rays, in radiotherapy these definitions have shifted over time. "Gamma ray" now indicates the product of nuclear decomposition (as in the obsolete Cobalt-60 machines) while "x-ray" denotes a flow of photons resulting from changes in an atom's electron orbits. In other words, my radiation would be the result of some shifting about of Tungsten electrons rather than an actual Einsteinian conversion of nuclear mass into energy. I know it's not rational, but this gave me a twinge of disappointment, as if there were something faintly less manly about not receiving *real* radioactivity.

I had already been in this room for some dry runs—"warm-up pitches"— that had been necessary before my actual treatments began. Just as misplaced ninth-inning fastballs can lead to walk-off homers, powerful beams of radiation require precise aim. Therefore I had been tattooed with two dots to properly align me with my customized "multileaf collimation" lead plate. This whole radiotherapy process was considerably more complicated than a mere chest x-ray, I soon surmised. High-energy photons travel more like a wind-blown swarm of unruly hornets than like a hail of parallel gunfire. Therefore, directing the right amount of them into my target flesh and having the right amount of their energy absorbed without causing excessive collateral damage necessitated the involvement of Berkshire Radiological Associates' team of white-coated physicists.

Radiation doses are measured in units called "grays," expressed in units of energy absorbed per unit of targeted flesh. A single gray translates into about a third of a foot-pound of energy per pound of human tissue. Dr. Gebara had decreed that I would receive twenty-six grays, fractionated into fourteen doses. (A curative dose of radiation *sans* prior chemotherapy would have entailed perhaps forty grays, as had been administered to my friend Janit S. a quarter-century before.) Each dose itself was divided in two, half through my chest and half through my back, in order to "cook" as little intervening tissue as possible with unnecessary exposure. Interestingly, rather than flipping me like a steak on the grill at the midpoint of each treatment, the giant transponder of the linear accelerator rotated 180° around me as I lay motionless and the frame of collimated lead plates accordingly reversed its configuration.

It was an uneventful 1-2-3 ninth inning... no runs, no hits, no baserunners. However, the radiation tired me out more than I thought it would. Like my chemotherapy, the side affects seemed cumulative. Dr. DeLeo's early wisdom was now much clearer— had I been treated with either chemotherapy or radiation alone, it would have been far more debilitating than the combination that I had just received. My final radiation treatment was on Friday, October 24. It was as brief and perfunctory a visit as most of them had been, except for the pink rose in a glass vase that the technicians sweetly presented to me as a "graduation" gift.

* * * * * * * *

Dr. DeLeo had also warned me that I might experience a psychological letdown of some sort as I made the transition from regular chemo and radiation treatments to a longer-term perspective on my post-malignancy well being. The cycle of chemotherapy infusions— enduring, processing, and then eliminating the quartet of poisons from my system every two weeks— had certainly afforded little room for pondering my future as a Canceroid. Likewise, the daily, ten-minute radiation appointments, though far less taxing than chemo, had provided an interesting distraction from such contemplative abstractions.

So, now what? I believe that I had at some point told everyone involved in my care, from Dr. DeLeo to the pulmonologist who tested my lungs, about my involvement in the sport of indoor rowing. But none of them, I suspected, had any inkling how suddenly and completely I would re-immerse myself in my athletic training the day after my final cancer treatment.

OVER THE RIVER... AND OVER THE HILL?

Over the river and thru the wood, to grandfather's house we go!
The horse knows the way... to carry the sleigh,
Through the white and drifted snow, oh!

Over the river and thru the wood, oh, how the wind does blow!
It stings the toes, and bites the nose,
As over the ground we go.

Over the river and thru the wood, to have a first-rate play;
Oh, hear the bell ring, "ting-a-ling-ling!"
Hurrah for Thanksgiving Day-ay!

Over the river and thru the wood, trot fast, my dapple gray!
Spring over the ground, like a hunting hound!
For this is Thanksgiving Day.

(Lydia Maria Child, 1844)

* * * * * * * * *

My five-month span of cancer treatments took me to the doorstep of November. For most of my life, this has been the most exciting month of my calendar year. Aside from my birthday, there was Thanksgiving, my favorite of all holidays. At different stages in my life I have also looked forward to Election Day, deer hunting season, and, more recently, to a season-ending college football game between bitter western Massachusetts rivals. Most importantly this time around, the approaching winter erg racing season meant that it was high time to start rowing regularly.

On October 25, the very next day after my fourteenth and final radiation appointment, I wholeheartedly flung myself into training for the World Indoor Rowing Championships. This event was scheduled for February 22, 2009, and would be hosted, as always, in Boston. With four months for whipping myself into shape, I figured, surely I could break the magical seven-minute barrier one more time. My muscles and organs had certainly taken a hellacious beating over the previous year, but my regular ergometer training would likely hasten their recovery.

The chemo- and radiation-induced diminution of my cardio-pulmonary capacity might even work in my favor, I optimistically reasoned, in a manner akin to high-altitude training. As I trained in my weakened state to make my muscles work harder and my bloodstream better able to supply them, my heart and lungs would concurrently strengthen from both the exercise and my healing process. By race day, my training and healing curves would intersect to great benefit, as if I had trained for a marathon at 7,000 feet and then returned to race in the oxygen-rich air at sea level. It was an interesting theory with at least some merit.

The fifth of November was my fiftieth birthday. I had never in my life done very much to mark the day, but being with Andrea would change this. In our on-line conversations in recent years, I had used her birthday as an excuse to perpetuate our communication. For this occasion, Andrea introduced me to the concept of the "birthday-month" by presenting me throughout November with small daily gifts… a tin of anchovies one day, a chocolate bar the next. In truth, I suspected she was slyly conditioning me for her own upcoming forty-ninth.

Reaching the half-century milestone used to constitute "over-the-hill" status. But many of my generation are the fortunate beneficiaries of scientific advances in nutrition and exercise, manage to work and play as energetically as we did in early adulthood. Accordingly, I rowed a total of 10,000 meters on the afternoon of November fifth, a prideful statement similar to my 5,000 workout right after my first chemo treatment. All I would need to do in order to race competitively in February was row long distances like this three or four times a week, with a day or two of hard sprinting thrown in.

＊ ＊ ＊ ＊ ＊ ＊ ＊ ＊ ＊

Although the NCAA football season kicks off before Labor Day, late autumn is prime-time for the great college rivalry match-ups. As the gold and crimson foliage give way to barren hardwood branches and the first inklings of winter, the traditional pigskin rivals get set to face each other at season's end. In all levels of college football, the fiercest enemies are often peas of a pod, schools that have far more in common with each other than with the other opponents on their schedules. Army and Navy, of course, make perfect gridiron combatants as they do battle in neutral Philadelphia every December. Likewise, Harvard and Yale annually vie in late November for blueblood bragging rights— and, in some seasons, the Ivy League championship.

In the frosty upper hollows of apple-pie-and-cheddar New England, however, the smaller, less-famous archrivals tend to square off several weeks earlier, usually on the second Saturday of November. And the greatest of these Division III college contests, a match-up that is even televised on regional cable each year, is the annual Williams-Amherst game. Like all of the other great football rivalries, this contest is personal, so genuine is the animosity between these two institutions. But unlike Army versus Navy or Harvard versus Yale, the Williams-Amherst tilt on November 8, 2008 would pit one ancient academy against its flesh-and-blood scion, as Amherst College was actually founded by a handful of defecting Williams faculty and students.

The "Biggest Little Game in America," as it bills itself, sometimes falls short of its hype. Back in 1995, Amherst and Williams contested a scoreless tie in drenching rain and half a foot of mud for what was perhaps the most boring sixty minutes of football ever televised. Running plays were fruitless pile-ups, passing impossible. Two years later, however, the two teams made amends. Williams bested Amherst 48-46 in a game remembered by many observers as one of the most exciting ever played at any level of football.

I had the pleasure of pacing the sideline that afternoon in late 1997 as Williams' kicking instructor. Our underdog Williams College Ephs unexpectedly broke out to a 21-7 early lead, but then the Lord Jeffs of

Amherst roared back, eventually stealing a 46-45 advantage on a trick-play two-point conversion with less than two minutes left in the game. The efficient and well-disciplined Williams offense then calmly marched three-fourths of the gridiron into field goal range, close enough for my freshman protégé kicker to convert his thirty-yard, last-second field goal attempt that sealed the dramatic two-point victory.

Eleven years later, going into the eighth and final week of the season, Coach Whalen's 2008 Eph squad boasted a record of five wins and two losses, identical to that of Amherst College. In 60° warmth and a light second-half drizzle, Williams edged their dreaded archrival 24-23... exactly half the score of that 1997 classic, with only a single blocked extra-point kick separating the winners and losers. I regretted being unable to attend the game in person with Andrea, for it would have been a great opportunity for her to personally experience Division III football at its purest, a form of excitement dearer to my heart than just about any other sport. But we were both needed at our jobs on the busiest day of the week in the food and wine trade. Maybe next year, I told her.

During the week after Williams' season-ending victory I continued to row, but then my lungs abruptly began to shut down. I was suffocating.

Dr. DeLeo's chemotherapy drugs had been very effective at killing my cancer cells. But by poisoning them as they did, they had also been expected to cause a degree of damage to my healthy tissue. My lungs, in particular, had taken a thrashing from the Bleomycin. "Pulmonary Fibrosis," i.e. scarring of the air sacs within the lung, is one of its known side effects. However, my last chemotherapy appointment had been over two months before... perhaps it was the radiation treatments? Dr. Gebara's photon beams had indeed been directed toward my upper rib cage.

Early in the week after the Williams-Amherst game, I phoned Dr. DeLeo's office to convey my concerns. I was experiencing an incessant, dry cough, with a terrifying sensation as if my lungs were stuffed with fiberglass insulation. I wasn't getting oxygen into my bloodstream in the manner to which I had been accustomed for the last fifty years, and had understandably taken for granted.

"Try to hold out until your Friday appointment," the BHO people told me. "But get to the emergency room if you feel you need to." I made it until Thursday night.

As soon as the Fairview Hospital emergency staff learned that I was a Canceroid, the red carpet was seemingly unfurled before me. Every possible courtesy and comfort was mine. By this time I had accepted as my duty to make people less uncomfortable around us Canceroids... even, surprisingly, employees in the medical arts. Once again I called upon my experience as a rower, putting the nurses and doctors a little more at ease by convincing them of my baseline good health with tales of ergometer racing. "Just a little speed-bump in my training," I courageously coughed to my Fairview caregivers. Of course I would be in Boston on February 22. There was still plenty of time to train.

Andrea and I left the emergency room after midnight with an anti-inflammatory drug, which was loaded into a plastic inhaler that I had trouble getting to work properly. I was able to get just enough medicine into my lungs to afford me a little sleep.

A few hours later, Dr. DeLeo examined me during our scheduled Friday morning appointment. He immediately ordered a high-definition CT-scan of my lungs that afternoon. If there was lung damage, he wanted to see it right away. Likewise, if this was the result of an infection, he needed to identify and eradicate it as soon as possible. As I rested in bed later that day, I was surprised and impressed that both Dr. DeLeo and Dr. Gebara personally phoned me to check on my status.

"Pneumonitis" was Dr. DeLeo's diagnosis after reviewing my CT-scan that same afternoon... pneumonia-like symptoms caused primarily by Dr. Gebara's radiation, he emphasized, not his Bleomycin. He sent me on my way with two prescriptions. Whether it was the steroid, or the antibiotic, or simply time, my lungs quickly returned to normal. By November 27— Thanksgiving morning of 2008— I was rowing as energetically as I had on my birthday, stroking a few thousand meters during a break from my kitchen duties.

* * * * * * * *

156

I have always loved Thanksgiving… perhaps because, in a way, it is the most childish of holiday feasts. As adults we rarely recall our yuletide menus of yore, as the presents beneath the tree are the primary purpose of Christmas to a youngster's mind. Furthermore, no single, signature entrée is broadly associated with Christmas dinner; one household has goose, its neighbor serves roast beef, and still another carves their second turkey of the year.

But the meal itself is the essence of Thanksgiving. Our earliest memories of its aromas and flavors thus remain with us forever, along with fond recollections of a houseful of rambunctious cousins and a gigantic, golden brown bird on the table. A wise Thanksgiving cook deviates from his traditional family recipes with extreme caution. It was only natural, however, that a lifelong restaurant professional like me would maybe experiment a little with variations on Thanksgiving's hidebound theme.

Over the years I had devoted considerable effort toward perfecting the turkey. In doing so, I came to the conclusion that it was foolish to roast a whole bird. After all, silky-tender filet mignon requires a vastly different cooking method than that used for sinewy stew meat, and thus roasting a whole side of beef would be as inappropriate as impractical. Likewise, the various parts of the turkey might best be cooked in different ways, I theorized. It took me a few tries before I got it right. This 2008 Thanksgiving dinner, I hoped, would showcase its final evolution.

A sit-down holiday dinner for sixteen, however, is too much for one cook to tackle alone, especially in someone else's home. Teamwork would be essential. We therefore divided cooking assignments among various family members, all of them mindful of holidays past.

Many of our family Thanksgiving traditions stemmed from my mother's mother. "Meema" Sullivan was a very good cook. After my family moved to the Rochester area in 1964, the highlight of our year was our annual return to the Berkshires in November to celebrate the holiday with her. We all had our favorite Meema dishes. I couldn't get enough of her pumpkin pie, and Sarah was especially fond of her mashed turnips. Everyone loved her simple and perfect bread stuffing.

My sister-in-law Yvonne, daughter of a former home-economics teacher, has been well-schooled in the kitchen arts and thus particularly adept at dessert-baking. Her pumpkin and apple pies will surely go down in family history alongside Meema's. None of us could match the fluffiness of our mother Mary's mashed potatoes... nor have we ever really tried, so long as she was available to make them. My sister Sarah's reverence for tradition extended to bygone dishes such as the once-ubiquitous bean and mushroom casserole. The trick to its success is in the pantry— canned beans, canned mushroom soup, even canned onion crisp for the topping. Use nothing natural or expensive— fresh *haricots verts* and wild fungi would render this preparation unrecognizable.

I was responsible for re-creating Meema's stuffing, an assignment that had required several previous holiday attempts. The trick, I eventually discovered, was to not over-think it... celery, onion, bread, a splash of stock, and Bell's pretty much did it. Salt, I found, was its friend, while fresh herbs tasted intrusive and unfamiliar. Meema's turnip dish was also simple and easy to make—so long as one didn't shy from adding butter, light cream, sugar, and salt. I was also responsible for the main course.

Turkey is a funny commodity. Though generally tastier, more nutritious, and less inexpensive than chicken, it finds its way into a family dinner only once or twice all year. Like candy corn and marshmallow peeps, turkey has become almost completely synonymous with one particular holiday to the exclusion of the rest of the year. This sharp annual spike in consumption makes for strange economics. While suddenly surging demand might be expected to drive turkey prices skyward, it is by definition a highly time-sensitive product. Unsold November birds are usually frozen until Christmas week. Many supermarkets, therefore, sell their Thanksgiving turkeys at zero profit in order to attract shoppers who will then fill their carts with all of the other holiday ingredients.

I had selected a pair of thirteen-pound turkeys earlier in the week. As a new Canceroid, I was all the more cognizant of the relationship between diet and health. If indeed the food we eat influenced our susceptibility to cancer, then one's choice of turkey mattered. Here were the options:

Major supermarket store brand, frozen...............................$.69/lb.

Major supermarket well-known brand.......frozen $.99/lb.; fresh $1.69/lb

Major supermarket lesser-known brand "Naturally raised"........ $1.29/lb

Major supermarket well-known brand "Naturally raised"......... $2.49/lb

Locally raised, organic, free-roaming, heritage-breed.............. $5.00/lb

Most mega-market brands of turkey are bred for massiveness of breast rather than flavor, inhumanely and chemically raised, even more inhumanely slaughtered, and then soaked with chemicals to replace the natural flavors that have been bred out of them... no thanks.

The local organic option, on the other hand, sounded especially Earth-friendly and healthy. This is how people *should* eat, a lot of us foodies sometimes find ourselves thinking or even preaching to others. However, mine was a value-added turkey recipe, a method by which the flavors of herbs, wine, and seasonings were steeped into the meat during several different cooking processes. Spending over $100 on totally natural, free-roaming turkeys only to have their expensive flavors obscured by my fancy cookery would be a waste. The lesser-known brand of "naturally-raised" turkeys— whatever that description actually meant— seemed like the best option.

I rose at 6:00AM on Thanksgiving morning and got right to work, comforted that getting the majority of the work done well ahead of the 2:00PM dinnertime would make the final hour before the dinner that much less stressful. Remi had flown in from Georgia on Monday, but unlike his sister he was of little utility in the hours before noon, so I let him sleep.

Sarah's kitchen was the heart of her home. I had cooked Thanksgiving dinner in it for the previous ten years or so, and it had become an especially important place for me in recent years. It was here where I delighted anew in home cooking as I took a rare, week-long vacation in July of 2006 while abruptly transitioning in mid-life from entrepreneur to clock-punching employee. It was in this very kitchen that Andrea and I had announced our wedding plans to my shocked family back in mid-February. Exactly six Sundays after that, I was again cooking a family meal in this kitchen when I paused to show my mother the puzzling new lump I had just discovered in my neck.

Although Sarah's kitchen was generously spacious, it was no more equipped for feeding large gatherings than kitchens in most other three-bedroom homes. For this 2008 dinner, we figured out a few shortcuts and improvements in advance. Positioning an island table in the middle of the huge kitchen would increase the working space, and then double as the buffet board for dinner service. My brother-in-law Jim agreed to fuel and fire up his outdoor grill— not for cooking, but rather to give us additional room to hold cooked food at the proper serving temperature.

Immediately after brewing a pot of strong coffee, I butchered the birds down into their fundamental sections— drumsticks from both leg and wing, breast (still on the bone), and thighs. I started a large stockpot flavored with onion, carrot, celery, fresh bay leaf, and Bell's Seasoning, in which I slowly poached the breasts for ninety minutes. One must be careful to keep them below a boil, which would immediately and irreversibly toughen the meat. As the breast meat slowly poached, I simultaneously roasted the backbones, wings, and necks on a cookie sheet. After withdrawing the finished breasts from their broth, I replaced them with these roasted scraps and then continued to simmer the pot.

As the churning turkey stock enriched itself, I browned the four thighs on all sides in a deep sauté pan while simultaneously preparing a fine dice of equal parts celery, onion, and carrot. I browned this vegetable mix and then combined it with the sautéed thighs in a large enamel braising pot, one of our wedding presents. To this I added red wine and turkey stock, along with a very un-Thanksgiving-like touch of tomato and garlic, the better to emulate classic *Osso Buco*. A tablespoon or two of demi-glace, though hardly a handy household ingredient, is a great way to add delightful richness to such long-simmered dishes.

NBC's coverage of Macy's annual parade droned in the background while I cooked. Although the musical numbers seemed electronically enhanced and perhaps intended for an older audience, it was a long-familiar component of Thanksgiving morning— as much a part of the day as Arlo Guthrie's famous anthem and the unmistakable kitchen aromas. The floats glided through Manhattan and acted as my timer for the turkey thighs as they gently braised at 325° for two hours. The breast meat, meanwhile, rested in the refrigerator, ready to be thinly sliced and then reheated on short notice by the addition of some of the boiling stock.

160

These very different cuts— the thigh and the breast— would both turn out fabulously moist and delicious. My method was working; only one thing was missing.

Ideally, Thanksgiving guests immediately catch a glorious whiff of familiar kitchen airs upon entering. And thus comes the third component of this Thanksgiving turkey system, the roasted drumsticks. Around mid-morning I began to roast the eight generously oiled drumsticks on the oven rack above the braising thighs for about an hour, and then I browned them beneath the broiler for five minutes or so. Their recognizable fragrance filled Sarah's home, and half of them immediately disappeared into the bellies of those in her household who had skipped breakfast.

At exactly 2:00PM the sixteen of us divided among three tables and raised our forks to the smoothest and most delicious Thanksgiving we had ever enjoyed. Left unspoken but probably obvious in everyone's mind was that I had much, much more to be thankful for than most. As this wonderful day dissolved into darkness and we all scattered from Sarah's home in our various vehicles, the miniature Thanksgiving that I had prepared for Andrea back in January seemed millions of miles distant. Marriage and cancer can do that.

Remi's flight back to Georgia was scheduled for so early on the following Monday that it was still headlight-dark as we hugged him goodbye at the airport in Westchester. Andrea and I then ventured into Manhattan to spend our day off taking in the holiday hoopla. To our disappointment, however, the sharply souring economy had spoiled much of the mood. The excitement over the recent presidential election had subsided, and financial gloom had dampened the usual post-Thanksgiving bustle.

However, November had always been my favorite time of the year, and even as the calendar advanced to December that day, I wasn't through enjoying the eleventh month's traditional pleasures. Now that my favorite holiday was a warm memory and our lives were back to normal, I would have time over the next few mornings to hunt… time to reclaim my place in the forests around a tiny village where I once answered to the nickname "killer."

SPENCERTOWN, NY

In my life I have called several different places home. For instance, I was born in the Berkshires of Massachusetts, where I now reside, and yet I grew from little boy to legal adult in an upstate New York town nearly three hundred miles away. After college I earned my restaurant chops during nearly a decade in Northampton, but Williamstown also fits me like old jeans, having spent so many afternoons there on a football practice field surrounded by the purple mountains. And of all these places, of all the little corners of my world that I have delighted in showing Andrea, I feel the most connected to the tiny hamlet of Spencertown, New York.

June B., the two-time ovarian cancer survivor and life-long family friend, has kept the same house there for nearly forty years. Dr. Robin T., a Medical School faculty psychiatrist, has lived across the street from her with his wife Anne and their huge clan for most of that time. As a young child I enjoyed whiling away summer days in Spencertown. June's house was a great place to just hang out and do little more than wade in the cool, spring-fed stream that meandered along her back yard's edge, or just observe indigenous wild creatures ranging from hummingbirds to wild turkeys. But Spencertown suddenly became a very different place for me as I entered my late teens.

Something completely unexpected happened to me right after my sixteenth birthday— my blood began to boil. It had nothing to do with Andrea, who was still a new and distant blip on my radar; rather, I was suddenly smitten by a powerful urge to hunt. At that point in my life I had no desire to spend any more time than necessary with my oppressive and somewhat maniacal father. But when he went out with my young brother on the opening day of the 1974 deer season and returned with two carcasses strapped to the roof of our family station wagon, an unfamiliar new bloodlust suddenly surged through my veins. I could think of nothing but deer hunting, and dreamed of it every night. Perhaps it was hormonal, an awakening of an ingrained instinct to feed oneself and others; maybe, therefore, the impulse to hunt is a survival mechanism buried deep within the brain, similar to a young teen's sudden obsession with the opposite sex that ultimately serves to perpetuate the species.

At the age of sixteen, however, I wasn't inclined to trouble myself with such complex and unanswerable questions. I just wanted to kill deer.

We planned my first hunt around our family's annual November trip to the Berkshires. My father, my brother, and I rose at 4:00AM on Thanksgiving morning and drove to Misery Mountain, right over the state border in Stephentown, New York. Deep in the forest around mid-morning, I discovered that I was blessed with the "eye of the hunter," able to pick out from the corner of my eye the partial silhouette of an unsuspecting little buck ambling through the thicket well below my trail. I was already a pretty good shot at that age, and an hour later we were driving home with this deer tied to our roof. I was hooked.

Two years later, I learned with great excitement that the three of us would have the opportunity to hunt with June's husband David in Spencertown, which we knew to be far more densely populated with deer than was Stephentown. David was a notoriously successful deer hunter in Columbia County. After he had more or less joined our family by marrying June in 1966, we soon learned of his legendary talents for separating fauna from their habitat, able to pull trout bare-handed from streams at summertime family picnics ("*hand-fishing*," he called it) and then fill whole barns with deer carcasses each autumn. Two days into the 1976 season, I was able to witness David the Deer Hunter in action.

We had taken up our positions in nearly total pre-dawn darkness, waiting for the deer to make their habitual morning trek from their swamp-side beds to higher feeding grounds. I was perched high in a fat old oak tree, with David standing a hundred or so yards away in the thicket below the large open field. He was invisible, as he never wore orange. "Best that other hunters don't see you at all," David repeatedly emphasized, clad always in colors of the forest and a funny-looking green felt hat.

163

As daylight crept across the landscape, a shot suddenly rang from David's rifle, a relatively low-powered .243 Winchester in deference to his chronic shoulder injury. Having missed a difficult shot, David yelled up to me— "HERE HE COMES!" A monstrous buck with a full rack of antlers stood hiding in the hedgerow below me. Between the thick branches I found his torso in my scope and squeezed the trigger.

The thunderous blast from my powerful .270 was many times louder than David's gun. Now David was hustling uphill through the open field as I climbed down from the tree, and my father and brother had also appeared on the scene. With all of us watching, the giant buck—which I was sure I had just killed— suddenly bolted from its protective hedgerow. David immediately fell to one knee and took aim. He wouldn't miss the same deer twice. A single syllable from his .243 somersaulted the mighty animal from its full sprint to the ground, instantly dead. I have never witnessed such a feat of field marksmanship before or since.

But David seemed to feel as bad for me as he was pleased with himself, sensing my deep disappointment that mine was not the lethal shot. After my father and brother returned home to Rochester on the Sunday after Thanksgiving, David suggested that he and I have another morning of hunting together, just the two of us.

It was snowing heavily that Monday as we took our familiar positions, and the young spikehorn buck that wandered up through the field that morning had a surprising amount of unmelted snow on its back. After I dropped it in its tracks with a single shot, it occurred to me that David must have let it pass by him. At first he denied this, but as he drove me back to my prep school that day he admitted that he had hidden behind a wide tree for safety as he waited for me to fire my rifle in his general direction. When I lamented the relatively diminutive size of the animal whose life I had just taken, David's immediate and simple response was one of life's most important lessons— "Gotta shoot'em when you see 'em," he firmly reasoned, "because you CAN'T shoot'em when you CAN'T see'em!" That same day, he half-jokingly nicknamed me "killer."

David and I spent many autumns hunting together, working as a team in the forest as one of us "pushed" the deer toward the other. During these seasons I had the opportunity to observe a man who had been born to hunt as surely as Beethoven had been born to compose his symphonies. David, I observed firsthand, could become one with the forest at will, invisible if he so desired. Deer have far more acute hearing and vision than humans, but David could somehow creep up to them undetected. And aside from his deadly accuracy with his little rifle, David had a God-given "eye of the hunter" that put mine to shame. One evening, as we drove home in pitch-blackness after a sunset hunt, David broke his usual stony silence in the pick-up truck. "See those three does back there?" Of course I hadn't, but how could he? His eyes had been focused on the dimly lit road ahead, I naturally assumed.

"What are ya, BLIND?" David teased as he abruptly turned the truck around and pointed to what must have been a dip in the field. There, barely visible, stood only the six *ears* of the three deer apparently standing in a deep swale. David wore glasses; I'd love to know who made them. During our many hunting trips David wasted few words, but I absorbed wisdom even from his silence. In particular, his deep love and respect for nature— even for the deer he relentlessly stalked and shot— were always evident in his deeds.

In November of 1993, David managed to shoot only a single deer. But this was, for him, a heroic accomplishment. For David had fallen gravely ill that autumn, and just three weeks later he was gone. It was pancreatic cancer that had stealthily overtaken David as no animal ever could. An overflow crowd packed the tiny church in nearby New Concord for David's memorial service, and everyone there recalled a different facet of this complex and enigmatic man beneath his deceptively simple demeanor. He was remembered from the lectern that afternoon as, among other things, a brave fireman, a skilled carpenter, a loving father, and an unlikely New York City college student while in his early thirties. I, of course, privately recalled him as a gifted hunter, the earthly offspring of Orion and Diana. If there were such a thing as an afterlife, I speculated that David's heavenly heath would be a teeming forest through which his ghost would forever and freely roam among his erstwhile quarry.

Along with David, so too during that winter of 1993 seemed to die my bloodlust for the hunt, as suddenly as its unexpected onset had drawn me to the forest nineteen years before. Meat-eater though I remained, I surrendered to the typical carnivore's hypocrisy— I could no longer raise a rifle to a fellow mammal and take full ethical responsibility for the food that I ate.

That God had chosen to so devilishly outfox a born hunter like David struck me as crueler yet than Beethoven's deafness. To what end would a supreme being pull such ill-humored pranks? And then, as if divinely admonished for such blasphemous wonderings, I suddenly found myself staring into the eyes of my own mortality in 2008 right after reuniting with Andrea.

David's widow had stared down probable death by Stage III ovarian cancer in 2005, and then endured its relapse in 2007. Accordingly, June was a natural source of comfort and wisdom as my definitive diagnosis gradually revealed itself. In between realizing that I in fact had cancer and finding out that mine was a relatively easily cured sub-type, June and I had reached an informal understanding. If I were to become deathly ill, I would spend my last months in the corner bedroom of her cozy Spencertown home, there to savor with my final respirations the piney perfume of her towering roadside evergreens, and then, by night, the soothing incense of her wood stove. How better to die? And were she to fall irretrievably sick before I did, then Andrea and I would move in and care for her. We would tend to her cats, take her for walks until she couldn't join us, and then lovingly close her eyes and tuck her in when she finally entered her well-earned rest after so many energetic and productive decades in this world.

* * * * * * * *

My fond memories of hunting in Spencertown extend beyond David. The rare camaraderie I shared with my father transpired during hunting season, and Robin T. and I had enjoyed a few memorable hunts together. Robin had shot his first deer during the 1981 season as we hunted (without David) the upper side of the choice parcel of woods owned by an elderly, German-born Jewish widow.

Mrs. Levi had known during her seventy-plus years the comforts of Old-World wealth as well as the horrors of the Holocaust. As Robin and I hilariously learned one morning, she had managed to maintain an excellent sense of humor through her many eventful years in this world.

It must have been about an hour after sunrise that day when I heard the unmistakable bark of the .30-06 rifle that Robin had borrowed from David. *Oh, no!* I thought— Robin had shot his fat four-pointer only a few dozen yards from Mrs. Levi's bedroom window. If she hadn't been awake, she certainly was now. We quickly field-dressed the animal, utilizing Robin's surgical experience as well as his scalpel and rubber gloves. Sure enough, Mrs. Levi appeared a few minutes later in her lavender bathrobe, just after we had hastily stuffed the animal into the back seat of Robin's vintage Volkswagen Beetle. "We'll never hunt here again," Robin and I mutually concluded as Mrs. Levi approached his vehicle, expecting her to be justifiably horrified at the grisly spectacle.

"*Zo,*" she began in her heavily-accented English, wagging her finger at the dead buck through the car window, "*if you are ze sonofabitch zats been eating my garden, I say, 'GOOD R-R-RIDDANCE! If not,*" she shrugged, "*vell, zose are ze breaks!*"

Sadly, in April of 2007 the Spencertown cemetery accepted for interment the third-oldest child of Robin and Anne T. after he succumbed to his esophageal cancer. Among his other accomplishments, thirty-one year-old Benjamin T. is fondly remembered by his multitudes of friends as a musician and sailor. Although he had not quite been born to the sea like, say, David to the forest, immediately after college Ben had adopted Neptune's realm as his campus, the tall-masted sailing ship as his graduate school dormitory.

During the weeks after Ben's wrenching demise, I took his younger siblings on several twilight deer-counting rides ("road-hunting") in order to get them out of their house and perhaps leaven their understandably heavy grief with a little amusement. The deer were still plentiful, as easy to find as ever. Then I got sick myself, and I finished my treatments right before the 2008 deer season opened.

Perhaps the road-hunting had rekindled something. I had just turned fifty, the same age as David when he shot his last deer. But his widow June and I were both emphatically alive, Canceroids united in survivorhood. Just like when I drove out to make Andrea dinner after so many years, another "long-dormant longing" of mine was rapidly awakening. For the first time since David's death, I felt a renewed desire to hunt deer again, to re-visit this significant aspect of my young adulthood and also share with Andrea yet another facet of my life.

David's premature passage in 1993 had extinguished my desire to hunt; maybe parting with this fundamental segment of my makeup had somehow brought me one step closer to my own mortality. Perhaps in some mysterious way I was more susceptible to getting sick myself after that. And so now, having beaten cancer (for the time being, anyway) maybe I was retracing this path in reverse... reconnecting with my inner hunter as my vital forces, my intertwined male impulses to copulate and hunt, regained in broad leaps their youthful intensity.

Male impulses... primitive, for sure, but one might charitably think of these as inborn inclinations to sire offspring, and then to take responsibility for feeding them. In a perfect world, these two forces would be connected; and if not, enforced as such by state child support guidelines. In any case, they are complementary forces psycho-biologically hardwired into the male brainstem, I suspect, ultimately beneficial to the perpetuation of the species. The lust-driven part, of course, is self-evident. Mature, responsible, males then feed their offspring via steady employment and grocery shopping. But to personally kill a living, breathing animal and then drag it home for dinner amounts to providing for the fruit of one's loins, the natural consequence of one's innate carnality, in the simplest sense imaginable.

Although I had just turned fifty, such abstract philosophical musings were as irrelevant to hunting at the half-century milestone as they were thirty-four years before. Once again, exactly like when I was a hot-blooded teenager, I just wanted to kill a deer.

* * * * * * * *

In the predawn lightlessness of Wednesday, December 3, my brother and I rendezvoused at June's house, just like we had so many times as teenagers with our now deceased father. Mrs. Levi, too, was long gone, but the new owners of her property kindly accommodated those of us who had traditionally hunted there. My old favorite hunting tree was now dead and mottled with rot, too unsafe-looking to climb. Instead I took a stand close by a thick tree several yards away. I patiently waited for the woods to absorb my intrusive entrance as the darkness dissolved into daylight and colors gradually emerged. One's eyes play tricks in the woods as daylight emerges, and the deer-like shape seventy yards away gradually revealed itself to be a leaf not far from my face.

But then, fully ninety degrees counterclockwise from my immediate attention, I clearly recognized a fragment of a familiar form as it emerged in the misty half-light. It had no horns, I could tell right away from a hundred yards through my binoculars... too small, too youthfully short of snout. But wherever such young fawns tread, a protective mother usually moseys nearby. And such a doe, particularly this time of year, might in turn be drawing the amorous attentions of a heavily-antlered buck or two, just as a beautiful but unsuspecting young high school girl might skew the paths of dozens of male schoolmates toward her hallway locker.

I had been getting a little cold sitting perfectly still, but nothing gets the warm blood pumping like the proximity of deer and the imminent possibility of a kill. I lost view of the fawn as it wandered into a thicket, but then, just a few minutes later, I heard an unmistakable noise on the other side of my stand, the sound of hooves prancing through twigs and leaves. There were six of them, two does with a pair each of fawns. I thoroughly examined each deer through my binoculars, but again I could see no horns. I waited perhaps fifteen more minutes, but no bucks followed them. This was a rather normal day of hunting in Spencertown, actually... lots of deer, but nothing to legally shoot. With so much excitement on such a warm and sunny day so late in the season, it was as perfect as an unproductive day in the woods could possibly be.

But still I yearned to fill my deer tag, and so I hunted again on Friday, Saturday, and finally Sunday, the hunting season's last day.

I needed to get to work at 10:00AM on Sunday, so I got an especially early start. It was still nighttime, really, as I fumbled and groped my way to the tree-stand by 6:00AM and waited for the first brushstrokes of morning light to pinken the southeastern sky. As they did, the forest became as sublimely beautiful as I've ever seen it— a light but steady dusting of snow was whitening the carpet of dreary brown leaves, lending depth of visibility to what was becoming before my eyes an oil-painted landscape. It was also, oddly, a warm snowfall, one that made the woods feel as soft and comfortable as the cashmere scarf caressing my neck. That not one deer came within my view was, ultimately, of little consequence. When it was time for me to leave for work, it was surprisingly hard to pull myself away. I got an inkling right then of how terribly difficult it must have been for David to pry himself from the forest at the end of what he probably knew was his last day ever of hunting.

With the soft, quiet ground as well as the increased visibility afforded by the fresh snowfall, it was conceivable that I might actually spy a shootable buck in the distance as I reluctantly covered the two hundred or so yards toward my car. I found myself pausing every ten paces or so, looking over my shoulder and back into the heart of the forest, hoping to catch a glimpse of a deer… or, just maybe, of a ghost in a green hat that surely must be wandering out there somewhere on this most beautiful of late autumn days. By nightfall the weather had dramatically shifted. Winter's howling blue breath was rudely erasing the day's comfortable beauty, turning soil to stone and rendering all of outdoors stingingly frigid and inhospitable.

At Christmastime I would be back with my Andrea to make the holiday rounds in Spencertown… my favorite home away from home, and a tiny rural paradise deeply scarred by cancer— as is any town or city, probably, if one looks closely enough.

BREAKING SEVEN

I must have looked pretty damn good during the week after Thanksgiving, because a lot of people had made a point of telling me so. My hair had been growing in nicely, and I was getting back into good physical shape, rowing as much as I could since the end of the radiation treatments. I had suffered through my touch of lung trouble in early November, but my breathing had cleared up enough to resume my rowing workouts again right before Thanksgiving, interspersed over the following two weeks with my hunting trips.

One doesn't automatically associate deer hunting with exercise, but an uninterrupted hour or so of walking through a soft-carpeted forest wearing heavy boots and clothing is surprisingly strenuous. Throw in nine pounds of rifle and a few steep hills, and one gets a genuine aerobic workout. All that plus the fresh air and the joy of returning to the hunt probably embellished my increasingly healthy glow with a touch of rosiness in my cheeks as well as the glint of renewed purposefulness in my eyes... the twinkle of a killer instinct, even.

I had hunted wisely and knowledgeably that week, and yet I hadn't come close to shooting a deer. This was another of life's important lessons that I had learned from David— you could do everything right on a given day and still not "succeed," per se. Life in general is like that. For instance, you can work hard for long hours and weeks and years, and then still lose your job without warning. Likewise, just about everyone, I imagine, has at some point tenderly offered his or her heart to another, only to be painfully rebuffed. Perfectly prepared soufflés sometimes fail to rise. Even well-kicked footballs occasionally miss the uprights because of random physical happenstance, through no fault of the kicker.

But there is a singular place within our broader world where effort is absolutely, directly rewarded, where there is no such thing as good luck or bad, and where one reaps exactly what one has sown, no more and no less.

The Concept2 Rowing Ergometer is the very essence of truth and fairness. It consists mainly of a sliding seat atop a horizontal beam along with a handle connected to a chain that, when pulled, rotates a flywheel with baffles that generate wind resistance. The harder you pull, the harder it pulls back, period. The most important component of the erg is the palm-sized, electronic "performance monitor" that measures, among other things, the speed of the virtual boat one is rowing through imaginary waters. Every bit of effort one expends on this elegant machine is quantified and displayed on the screen... and the ergometer never lies.

Whether training or racing, the most important number on the performance monitor is the instantaneous pace. With each stroke, this figure is expressed as the time (in exact minutes and seconds) that would elapse rowing five hundred meters with strokes of identical power. The lower this figure, therefore, the harder (and faster) one is rowing. The pace necessary to row two thousand meters in exactly eight minutes would be expressed as two minutes per five hundred meters... 2:00/500m as read on the performance monitor. When I'm in shape, I can "pull 2:00's" for nearly a full hour. Rowing a two thousand meter race in seven minutes flat, however, would necessitate average pulls of 1:45.0.

An erg race is a remarkable sight— a gym-ful of these contraptions, with wave after wave every fifteen minutes or so of men and women, boys and girls, grouped by sex and age and rowing their hearts out. I had competed in a handful of erg races over the past two decades. And although early in my forties I had pretty much forsworn further competitions, I had kept myself in nominally competent erging condition in recent years, even while operating two time-consuming food businesses. But then, back on New Year's Day of 2006, two years before reuniting with Andrea, I was suddenly inspired to re-enter the ring, as it were, by an unlikely meeting with an extraordinary female athlete.

In late 2005, I had just started to meet interesting women on-line in the evening hours after working my usual long days. During an especially busy dinner shift on one of the last nights of that December, a petite, dark-haired woman appeared in my restaurant doorway and boldly introduced herself. Although she and I had been e-mailing back and forth for the previous two weeks, I was unable to recognize her as the "Susan" with whom I had been corresponding. This was because she was far more attractive in person than in her on-line photos... the exact opposite of most of my Internet dating experiences. I'd be calling her VERY soon, I assured her.

"Got any plans for New Year's Eve?" I asked her on the phone two days later.

Well... no, she hadn't made any. "But aren't you working really late?" she understandably wondered.

"Yeah, but its always midnight *somewhere*... I'll bring the champagne." It was not my style to expect to sleep with a complete stranger, she was relieved to hear me volunteer.

Our atypical first date began about half an hour after the Times Square ball had dropped, and lasted nearly until dawn. It was a night of lame TV and fun conversation. On New Year's Day of 2006, we awoke from perhaps two hours of innocent napping on her sofa in lieu of a proper night's sleep. Upon arising and brewing us coffee, Susan perkily announced that she felt energetic enough to run a scheduled twenty-kilometer race through that morning's bitter cold and snow in preparation for her Boston Marathon attempt in the spring. *What the fuck?* I wondered— was this chick *bionic* or something?

Although she didn't look it, Susan was nearly four years older than me, and therefore she had nearly completed high school when Title IX of the Education Amendments of 1972 came along and (theoretically) opened the doors of interscholastic athletic competition to females. After weeks of being alternately shunned and contemptuously belittled by her high school's track coach, Susan— who could outrun most of the boys in her school— had stood at the starting line of the suddenly co-ed hurdles competition of her first meet. She cleared the first two hurdles, but then she caught her foot on the third and promptly fell face-first into the cinders, painfully embedding them into her palms and knees. Thus did Susan's track career ignominiously end until many years later, when her innate athleticism and relentless drive found an outlet in marathon running. The 2006 Boston Marathon would be her fourth race at that distance.

My relationship with Susan never evolved into anything beyond friendship and mutual respect after that unforgettable meeting. But I was sufficiently inspired by her energy and determination on that New Year's Day morning to take up serious erg racing again. There was a competition scheduled just forty days hence— the 2006 Adirondack Sprints at Rensselaer Polytechnic Institute (RPI) in nearby Troy, New York. Maybe— just maybe— there was enough time to whip myself into good enough shape to break seven minutes for 2,000 meters. Seven minutes was the magical milestone that separated hard-core rowers in my age division from the multitudes of half-serious exercise buffs. Breaking seven minutes required many long hours of lonely and painful training. For someone my age and weight, it would be an admirable badge of honor. But to achieve this goal on such short notice, I needed to subject myself to a Manhattan Project-like crash-training regimen.

Erg racing demonstrates that the human body is like a hybrid-fuel automobile, powered by different metabolic pathways depending on its needs. All human muscular activity ultimately relies upon the breakdown of adenosine triphosphate (ATP), which is continuously generated from the body's reserves of nutrients. Stored body fat is loaded with calories, but requires too much oxygen to utilize it for anything more strenuous than, say, walking through the woods in hunting gear. Carbohydrates, though less laden with available energy, are more readily usable for slightly more vigorous endeavors, such as Susan's distance running. And when one requires an especially high rate of energy output, as when rowing at full speed, the body is able to meet such demands for brief periods by burning stored carbohydrates without oxygen. This process, known as anaerobic metabolism, is highly inefficient and generates a painful build-up lactic acid in the muscles as a by-product.

For the first ten seconds or so of an erg race, the muscle cells require no oxygen to perform work; rather, they rely first upon perhaps three seconds' worth of stored ATP, almost like starter fluid for a cold automobile engine. Creatine phosphate is then briefly available in the muscles for re-synthesizing ATP, lasting another seven seconds or so before oxygen finally becomes necessary. During this initial segment of a race the erg racer wisely sprints at full speed in order to take advantage of these stored fuels, which would otherwise go unutilized.

After this brief burst of energy, the erg racer then settles into a slower race pace and relies upon his circulatory system to provide enough oxygen for the ATP process in the working muscles. But after a few minutes at race pace, the rower's muscles are demanding more oxygen than even a well-trained heart and lungs can supply. In response, like a fighter jet firing up its afterburners, the muscles switch over to the anaerobic pathway. And just as the jet screeching through the sky at maximum speed quickly depletes its fuel, the erg racer can only operate like this for a few minutes before crashing.

Knowing all of this as I prepared for my race, my erg workouts were a mix of aerobic pieces (long distance work without going into oxygen debt) and anaerobic wind sprints that agonizingly trained my muscles to do more work with less oxygen. Either way, these training sessions left me completely exhausted and drenched with sweat, my legs wobbly and my lungs burning. And yet, even as I knelt on the gym floor in pain, desperately gasping for oxygen, it also felt strangely euphoric. After a few days of this I became so addicted to the pleasurable endorphins released during such exertion that a missed workout probably would have felt like opiate withdrawal.

As Race Day drew near I clearly understood, as did the other entrants, I'm sure, that no one would win any races on that day itself, strictly speaking. These races will have already been won or lost in the previous months of training, and every rower would know within a few seconds what his or her time would likely be. Races such as this, therefore, were like conventions at which like-minded erging enthusiasts proudly displayed the fruits of the discipline to which they had subjected themselves. As such, the erg race is the carrot that makes us willing to apply the stick to ourselves in preparation.

As for me, my race was against the clock alone. I was in the midst of training non-stop for forty days, pushing myself so hard through so much pain to break the seven-minute milestone that I had begun to hate the number seven itself. This was personal. If I could just keep my overall race pace below 1:45, I figured, I would win everything I had trained for and I didn't care who else won what. Seven minutes... seven minutes of total hell, and then it would be over.

Finally, it was my Race Day— February 11, 2006. I had grudgingly come to accept, to my great disappointment, that I would not be able to make my goal. Forty days had simply not been enough time to whip myself into that kind of shape. I had hit the wall, I concluded a week before the race after another disappointing time trial. My times were stuck, and I hadn't really improved appreciably after my second week of training.

But although the ergometer, as I have noted, rewards one's efforts nearly tit-for-tat and therefore makes one's race result fairly predictable, there is another element to the sport, a variable that makes race day a little more interesting. As in many other sports, the crucible of actual competition is different enough from the lonely and painful hours spent in training so as to reveal aspects of human character previously unseen in practice sessions.

The most intense competitors in all manner of sport relish rather than fear the moment of truth. NFL place-kickers, for example, live for the last-second game-winner, and NBA superstars for the final, do-or-die jumper in Game 7. Likewise, Race Day inspires the best erg racers to push themselves a little beyond their known limits. One often cannot help but pull harder and faster when everyone is watching, and quitting is unthinkable, even as one stews in lactic acid accumulation that feels like fire flaying one's flesh from the bones. As such, the erg race itself is like a rite of passage, a ritual not unlike Kwai-Chang Caine excruciatingly cradling the scorching hot urn of embers to facilitate his exit from the Shaolin temple; or, even, my black belt test, during which my *sensei* intentionally fractured my ribs in order to see whether I was willing and able to fight while thus injured.

And so there I was in the gym at RPI on February's second Saturday of 2006... ready to demonstrate the limits of my ability for all to see, upon the machine that never lies. My sister would also be racing, so this would be a family affair. Her husband Jim, a collegiate rowing coach, had agreed to share his expertise and talk me through my race. "What's your plan?" he asked me.

"I'm trying to crack seven," I responded, in our familiar erg racing shorthand. "But realistically I don't think I can. So I'll pull 1:46's and 1:47's for 1400 meters. Then if I have enough left, I'll start pulling like hell and go for it. Otherwise I'll just coast in and try to beat 7:10."

Naturally, my plan went out the window as soon as the race began.

Around one o'clock, the tournament director announced that the men's masters (i.e., the old guys, 40-49) were up next. We were a mix of area rowing coaches, husbands of female rowers, and me, nine of us in all. I silently prayed for the strength and courage to do my very best as I dropped to one knee beside my designated machine and ritualistically knotted my black belt around my waist. I only wear it for erg races, and, if nothing else, it would remind me not to quit in the face of pain, remind me that I had once been able to fight with broken ribs. Then I strapped myself in and adjusted my settings, visualizing the race before me and mentally dividing it into three two-minute segments. By doing so, the race— and the pain— would seem more manageable.

It would also prevent me from thinking about the race's horrible final minute until it was actually upon me.

I needed to get a good hard start so that my overall pace would come down to my target pace early on and I wouldn't need to play "catch-up" for very long. Having to pull harder than my target rate for very long would strain my muscles, and perhaps I would need them at the finish. But for something so difficult and painful, the first two minutes were relatively easy. I found myself going too fast— I actually had to resist pulling

1:43's, perhaps because of Race Day adrenaline. Coach Jim convinced me to conserve my energy, and I met him halfway. But still I felt an unfamiliar floating sensation as I rowed, as if watching myself from outside of my body. I honestly couldn't feel the pain that I knew I was in.

Going into the second two-minute segment I still felt unusually good, though I darn well understood that I was running up a stiff oxygen tab, burning more than I inhaled on each stroke as my pace crept up to 1:44. As I rowed through this segment, Coach Jim kept reminding me to settle down, that I was going faster than I had planned. Indeed, adrenaline is often an enemy during this part of a race, fooling one into pulling a more aggressive pace and then cruelly abandoning one's limp, spent body well short of the finish. But I was still feeling better than I should, though in reality I was really doing nothing more than rowing to the starting line of the third and by far the most difficult segment. I felt more than a little afraid at this point, because I knew that I wasn't exactly paddling into the tunnel of love... this was going to hurt like hell.

Segment three began with about eight hundred meters to go. Coach Jim and the rest of my family, sensing my increasing exhaustion and pain, started to shout words of encouragement. I was pretty sure at this point that I could meet my goal, so long as I was able to endure the imminent onslaught of agony. But then my body's warning lights started to flash, telling me that I was dangerously low on fuel. My muscles, meanwhile, were suddenly descending from anaerobic purgatory into the flames of hell, and they were going to start defying orders from my brain sometime very soon. Every cell in my body was suffocating, crying out for oxygen, and only through sheer force of will could I continue rowing through such discomfort. But I kept counting my strokes in quartets and watching the monitor, straining to maintain my target pace and reminding myself that it would be over very soon. Meanwhile my advantage beneath 1:45.0, the seven-minute pace, was steadily melting away. I honestly didn't know if I could maintain it much longer as the sixth minute expired.

And so what about the final minute that I had intentionally neglected to consider? This unaccounted-for segment worked out to be a little less than three hundred meters, certainly a significant proportion of the race. Well, erging is often a family sport, with wives and husbands commonly entering tournaments together in their respective divisions. And as the wives often fondly shout during their husbands' races—

"C'mon, honey! You can do ANYTHING for one minute!"

For that final minute, the erg racer has nothing left but the fumes in his empty tank, his pride, and his ability to withstand pain. It is the longest minute in a rower's life.

With two hundred meters left, the lobe of my brain in charge of exertion threw in the towel, but I refused to stop fighting. I would surely have quit right then had I been rowing a practice piece, but I hadn't trained as hard as I did to just meekly surrender this close to the finish. Besides, I was wearing my black belt, which perhaps gave rise to my hallucination of my *sensei* tauntingly screaming in my face as I rowed—

"Are you tired? Are you TIRED?"

I could clearly envision his frightening face just inches from mine, his eyes like blue lasers and his neck veins menacingly engorged.

"NO, SENSEI!!" I automatically responded, perhaps aloud, or maybe just to myself.

Fifty meters later I slowed my stroke rate a little and pulled correspondingly harder, calling upon my leg and back muscles to pick up the slack from my exhausted heart and lungs. The flywheel screamed and then sighed with each of my deliberate, exaggerated strokes, but my monitor showed that my average pace had crept up to 1:44.9. Could I hold the line? My oxygen debt had reached my credit limit, and my muscles wouldn't let me borrow any more. I watched my remaining meters mercifully dwindle like sand in an hourglass— ten, five, ZERO! Coach Jim quickly pressed a button on my clock to find my official time...

I DID IT! By less than a second! The men's masters' heat at the 2006 Adirondack Sprints had required only six minutes and fifty-nine-point-four seconds of hell after all. I crawled off the machine and remained panting for air on the floor for a few minutes, unable to stand. Though my legs were useless jelly and my lungs felt as though I had just power-chained a pack of unfiltered Camels, I had vanquished my seven-minute foe, and I was in heaven.

I had entered a handful of indoor regattas in years past, so I more or less knew what I was getting myself into at RPI. But this 2006 race was different. Never before had I mysteriously transcended erg racing's intrinsic agony to sense my soul afloat in a state of otherworldly peacefulness. I felt somehow detached from my mortal body, watching it from above as it rowed. This experience forever changed me, and I was hooked. Just like when I had shot my first deer, just like when I had first spied young Andrea, I was deeply, permanently hooked. Going forward, I would be a rower-monk of sorts, finding the Divine in the Concept2's performance monitor. Every future erg competition would be more than just a race— it would be a passage, a spiritual rite of transforming the impossible into something doable.

A year later I was out for even greater glory. I took first place in the 2007 Adirondack Sprints as well as the meet hosted by the Hudson River Rowing Association in Poughkeepsie, raising in the process a total of $4,000 in charitable pledges for the Cardinal Hayes Home for Children. Unsettlingly, however, my race times had been only slightly better than the year before in spite of many more months of diligent training. There was an unfamiliar clutching sensation in the center of my rib cage as I rowed, because my as yet undiscovered tumors were apparently competing for chest capacity with my lungs. I never quite got in sync for the indoor rowing season of early 2008. The endurance that had previously won gold medals had mysteriously abandoned me.

And now, in the midst of the 2008 holiday season, I was cancer-free and eagerly anticipating and training for the 2009 C.R.A.S.H.-B. races. This would be the perfect forum for demonstrating my complete recovery with one final sub-seven-minute effort— a resounding "FUCK YOU!" to my illness and all it had done to me during the preceding year.

I would indeed make it to Boston for the big race, but not at all in the manner that I had expected.

AND THE WINNER IS...

Like my previous Guido's yuletide seasons— and, of course, my recent months of cancer treatments— the run-up to Christmas of 2008 tested the reserves of my energy and strength. But then suddenly in the midst of my annual holiday exhaustion it was Christmas Eve itself, a brief respite from the stress. I wanted to make Andrea a special dinner for the occasion, and so it was once again time to call upon my years in the trenches of the restaurant business. Among the many talented cooks in the restaurant-rich Massachusetts city of Northampton, where I had worked for a decade after college, one stood out as especially talented and inspirational.

Chef Michael was an astrophysicist by training who had later ventured into the culinary arts because, as he put it, "cooking was a more direct path to enlightenment." For a chef, Michael was uncharacteristically cerebral and slight of build. He was also evidently wealthy enough to have been able to work for peanuts under a series of old-school French chefs while absorbing enough know-how to eventually captain a kitchen himself.

Michael's menu never strayed far from the classical French repertoire, eschewing the silly extremes of *nouvelle* cuisine so voguish in the mid-1980's. His somewhat by-the-book classical cookery also pre-dated the wholesale Mediterranean reinvention of American fine dining, with its extra-virgin olive oil and sun-ripened everything, that would almost completely displace traditional French fare like his just a few years hence. Northampton in the Reagan years was a prosperous, party-like scene, and thus a nurturing cradle of culinary sophistication. Chef Michael was definitely in the right place at the right time, and I was very fortunate to have been there with him.

From soups to desserts, every dish Chef Michael painstakingly executed was as perfectly delicious as I could possibly imagine it. (It was Michael who had collaborated with me to perfect and serve my idea for a poached oyster dish.) But just as he had stood out among his Northampton kitchen peers, one of his creations became my clear favorite. It was, for a chef so classically trained, an unusually creative appetizer— "Ragôut of Escargots, Wild Mushrooms, & Preserved Duck," as it read on the menu of a forty-seat micro-*boîte* where we had briefly worked together before I enticed him to follow me to a larger French restaurant up the street.

The fungi weren't exactly wild— shiitake mushrooms, as ubiquitous in the eighties as portobellos would later become in the Italy-obsessed nineties, were generally cultivated rather than hunted. And the "preserved duck" was old-school French *confit*, which Michael prepared from scratch over the course of several days. He used the term "ragôut" to indicate a hastily assembled stew, sautéed rather than long-simmered. A rich red wine sauce enhanced with demi-glace united this culinary ensemble, which Michael served with plain toast points and modestly garnished with a toss of parsley.

On one stormy winter night in early 1984, Michael and I had watched a famous opera singer lovingly savor every bite of his Ragôut in our otherwise empty dining room. But people rarely cooked or ate like this anymore. Today very few restaurants even attempt such ambitiously exquisite fare, except perhaps in castle-like gourmet destinations where one might dine for three hours, drop triple figures per person, and then snore the night away upstairs in an antique poster bed.

That being said, I like to think I'm a pretty decent cook, capable of accurately co-opting ideas from the many talented chefs with whom I have worked over the years. And so for my first Christmas Eve with Andrea, this dish would make a great main course, I imagined, simply by serving it over a four-ounce "platform" of pan-seared beef tenderloin. It would thus become a variation, really, of Tournedos Rossini. Armed with the memory of Chef Michael's masterpiece and the knowledge and experience to at least approximate it, I got to work in our Great Barrington kitchen, just as I had in her Penfield home back on that magical afternoon in early January at the other end of this same year.

After sautéing a fine dice of carrot, celery, and leek in butter, I added a minced clove of garlic and stirred for another minute before pouring in a glass of red wine. About ten minutes of gentle simmering later, a tablespoon of demi-glace, a swirl of butter, and a little salt and pepper were all that was necessary to approximate Michael's sauce. I was able to purchase decent-quality *confit* at Guido's, as well as the fresh shiitakes and canned snails. I sautéed each of these three components separately before adding them to the sauce as the tenderloin browned in my favorite iron frying pan.

For such a complex-sounding dish, it was downright easy to prepare and quite delicious. Andrea appreciatively devoured it with unselfconscious gusto, just like that opera singer a quarter-century before. And yet there was room for improvement, I decided. Next time I should place a crispy potato pancake beneath the tenderloin, and also seek out the smaller, *petits gris* type of snail rather than the fatter and blander type more commonly available in gourmet supermarkets.

We began our first Christmas Day together with a few cozy and relaxing hours at the home of my brother and his family in nearby East Greenbush. On the way back to Great Barrington, we stopped to visit Robin T.'s clan in Spencertown. As the faint Christmas Day sun dipped behind the undulating hills of Columbia County, Andrea and I took seats at Robin's dinner table in their crowded little dining room. Robin immediately poured us some wine, a natural and effortless gesture of hospitality for having included him in our holiday rounds.

"Wait," I interrupted as he was about to show me the label. "Don't tell me what it is."

This was a little game that I often played with my wine salesmen. Tasting their samples blind, I could more often than not give them the country of origin, the grape variety, and the retail price within a dollar. It was an entertaining way to keep my salesmen as well as myself more honest about our business. Robin poured us each a glass of red wine— cold, right from the refrigerator— and I inhaled deeply as I tried to warm the glass with my hands to help it open up and better reveal its mysteries.

"Is it French?" I asked. "This tastes French." If not, it could be too many different things for me to accurately nail— a varietal Merlot from Chile? A New World-style Argentinean? No… this wine was definitely French. Guessing wines blind like this is fraught with potential humiliation. Thirty years ago the average wine maven might have easily gotten this one, mainly because there were so few other possibilities. But now there was so much decent wine produced in so many different countries that one might easily be embarrassingly wrong by a continent, an ocean, or a hemisphere.

"Uh, yeah… it IS French," Robin replied in curious disbelief. Whatever region of France it was from, it tasted to me like about twelve bucks retail. It was either a Côtes-du-Rhône, an inexpensive Bordeaux, or maybe a stray drop from the sea of decent, cheap wine produced in the Languedoc. I searched my vast and hard-earned banks of taste memory for guidance. Was this wine Mediterranean-tasting, or more continental? Did the fruit flavors conjure imagery of warm colors, or soothingly cool shades? Were the tannins hard, or dusty?

I swirled another sip, warming it in my mouth. Aha! Suddenly I recognized the signature nuance that mere language cannot fully describe, a unique nexus of fruit, minerality, and man's handiwork that, once detected, betrayed this wine's exact provenance. "This wine is a *cru bourgeois* Bordeaux," I accurately declared, to everyone's astonishment. Truth be told, this particular wine was easier than most for someone in the wine business to nail; I could imagine Chef Michael somehow identifying it *over the phone*. But this feat always seems impressive to purely recreational wine drinkers.

As the bottle slowly drained, we found ourselves spending a late afternoon hour fondly reminiscing about family and friends who had left us— Mrs. Levi, David, and, of course, Ben— almost as if they had all re-materialized from the past to join us for the holiday gathering.

Once we finally got back to our apartment, our cumulative holiday exhaustion immediately dragged us off to sleep. Our Christmas Day of 2008 had been little more than a brief break from our employment. Between Andrea's long waitress shifts and my overtime hours at Guido's, there had been precious little time to even recognize the holiday and its powerful meaning, much less celebrate it. Very soon— *too* soon, it seemed— we were right back at work.

After another full-throttle week at the seafood counter, it was New Year's Eve, with its attendant orders for hundreds of pounds of shrimp and dozens of lobsters and oysters. Then New Year's Day dawned, signaling the abrupt end of our busy stretch. It was time to kick my ergometer training into high gear for the upcoming racing season, just as I had for my crash training regimen back in 2006. I rowed and rowed in early January... lengthy pieces and short; intervals, and great distances. Soon my leg muscles became thicker and more sculpted, and a sextet of rocks emerged from my mid-section. I could feel myself beginning to progress ever so slightly toward my race-day target times.

* * * * * * * * *

The perfect ending to my year-long battle with cancer would be for me to have trained, Rocky-like, into fabulous rowing shape, and then to have dramatically broken the seven-minute mark one last time at the 2009 C.R.A.S.H.-B.'s. This would have felt like crumpling cancer itself to the canvas with blow after bruising blow to its abdomen and jaw. Since the completion of my treatments I had spent about two months thus far training for such an outcome, regularly visualizing myself rowing the final, painful strokes of my triumphant race against the clock.

Around mid-January I hit the usual wall in my training. My times were stuck. This was typical, I understood; training for erg racing usually entailed periods of steep improvement interrupted by frustratingly flat stretches. But this was different... this time I was unable to row faster than 2:00/500m for any significant distance. Most unusually for me, it seemed as though I couldn't even muster the requisite endurance to train hard enough to improve. What the hell was going on?

I experienced waves of anger, fear, and then sadness as I grudgingly absorbed the truth— that I was physically unfit to compete in any erg races this season. No amount of determination or effort, no competitive glint in my eye, or even a black belt knotted about my waist could alter this stone-cold reality. The poisonous chemicals and destructive photons hurled into my corpus by Drs. DeLeo and Gebara, the Ace and the Closer of Berkshire County's exemplary anti-cancer staff, had exacted too great a toll upon my heart and lungs. They would require a much longer recovery than was necessary for my hair to grow back. Alas, I was no Sampson.

Maybe next year, I told myself. But maybe in truth I would never be able to race again. The damage to my lung capacity, my ability to infuse oxygen into my blood and thus my muscles, might well be permanent. This further saddened me… it made me feel as though cancer had actually succeeded in killing a part of me, that I had forever lost something of great personal value. I felt diminished. But as readily as I contemplated such thoughts, I realized that they were incredibly selfish. All I had to do was look around me to realize how lucky I was in so many ways.

It wasn't so long ago that tombstones were regularly engraved with the epitaphs of otherwise healthy young people who had perished from Hodgkin Lymphoma. I had been the fortunate beneficiary of its state-of-the-art cure, almost entirely paid for by my employer's insurance company. Instead of brooding over the loss of my ability to race competitively, I should have been thankful that rowing had so thoroughly prepared me— physically *and* spiritually— for facing cancer in the first place. Emerging from this challenge as a fully initiated yet healthy Canceroid more than justified this sacrifice. Likewise, if Hodgkin Lymphoma was indeed the "grand karmic counterbalance" of my reunion with Andrea, then I think I got an especially favorable deal.

I had many blessings worth counting, I realized… especially when I considered the plight of friends and neighbors less fortunate than I—

Throughout all of my years at the Lenox Fitness Center, there had been a much older member who rowed almost as often as I did… though at a seemingly snail-like pace whenever I was waiting for a machine. "Old Sam" was in his mid-seventies, and he wore twenty years' worth of battle scars from his multiple encounters with cancer. He was "sick again," as the gym managers explained it... really bad this time. I had seen Old Sam and his relatively young wife at the chemo salon during one of my treatments, and he had looked frail and tired. He hadn't been to the gym in a while, and his prognosis was bleak.

In October of 2008, yet another close family friend had been diagnosed with cancer. Ann M. had grown up with my mother in Pittsfield and therefore had known me since birth, like June B. had. Ann had lived a deeply religious life, so much so that local priests regarded her with a measure of respect seldom extended to the laity. She was generally regarded to have important connections "upstairs." If so, she was going to need them, for Ann M. had been diagnosed with pancreatic cancer, the same malignancy that had robbed us of David.

And then there was the amazing story of Anna O.

With the aid of a popular social networking website, I had been keeping an ever-expanding circle of old friends informed of my medical status. This provided some unexpected benefits. While in bed with my laptop after one of my infusions, I reacquainted myself to an entire family with whom I had lost contact after high school. The father, Dr. G., had been our family doctor back in Ontario, and his children were our Wayne Central schoolmates. One of the doctor's grandchildren, I soon learned, had fallen suddenly ill with cancer a few years before.

Though a teenager, Anna O. had been diagnosed with neuroblastoma, a cancer that almost always strikes babies and is nearly uniformly fatal within a year. Thanks in part to Dr. G.'s early detection and Anna's years of intensive treatments, she has remained healthy and strong through seven *years* of hell, qualifying her as some sort of living miracle.

In addition to the numerous rounds of chemotherapy and surgeries she has had to endure, Anna O. has willingly subjected herself to every experimental protocol available in order to provide neuroblastoma researchers with a rare and valuable adult subject for their clinical trials. By continuing to do so in spite of the side effects and frequent hospitalizations, Anna is helping to save the lives of babies in the future. She has also established her own charity for neuroblastoma research funding.

Unlike the typical Hodgkin Lymphoma patient, Anna O. knows that her good fortune could run out at any moment, that her sunny days might darken with very little notice.

* * * * * * * * *

With so much to be thankful for, Andrea and I decided that our "Second Annual Super Bowl Eve Wine Tasting" would not be a fundraiser, but rather a gesture of appreciation to those who had taken care of me— the staffs of Berkshire Radiological Associates and Berkshire Hematology & Oncology.

Shelley W., a talented catering chef as well as the proprietress of Haven Café & Bakery, lent us the use of this swank downtown Lenox restaurant for the evening. She also insisted on showing off some of her food to our guests. My favorite wine supplier donated the necessary bottles, and he and I talked our gathered guests through the various wines as we fielded their questions. Just like our tasting the year before, everyone seemed to have a great time, and the gathering gave Andrea and me the chance to offer our sincere thanks to everyone who had saved my life.

But I still wanted to do my usual winter fundraising for a worthy charity, and once again the Concept2 ergometer was the vehicle.

On the morning of February 22 we drove the two hours to Boston for the 2009 C.R.A.S.H.-B. World Indoor Rowing Championships, the Super Bowl and Daytona 500 combined of this relatively obscure and humble sport. Maybe I should have seen it coming, but upon suddenly spying Boston University's cavernous Agganis Arena filled with scores of brand-new ergometers as well as thousands of fellow indoor rowers from around the world, I was emotionally staggered for a moment. Immediately before us stood a hockey rink full of hard-core erg racers from around the world. The Harvard Crewmen were out in force, as were Olympians from as far away as China and Poland. There were also lots of regular rowers like me, I could tell, fellow rowing nuts who shared my close familiarity with the sport's intrinsic loneliness and pain as well as its hard-earned rewards. I felt left out.

But getting to know Anna O. had given me an idea that lent an alternative purpose to our presence in Boston that day. During the previous two winters I had generated charitable contributions through my erg racing and wine tasting for the Cardinal Hayes Home. In the winter after my bout with cancer, I would instead raise money for Anna's cancer charity, I had decided... by raffling off an ergometer, since I wouldn't be racing myself. For the contest's prize, Andrea and I had arranged in advance to purchase a nearly new machine from the C.R.A.S.H.-B. organizers, used out-of-the-box new for the competition. With considerable effort and ingenuity, we were able to maneuver the machine into my little Hyundai and bring it back to the Berkshires.

* * * * * * * *

A few days after the race I was back on an ergometer at the Lenox Fitness Center, rowing as hard as my chemo- and radiation-scarred lungs would permit. At most gyms, rowers go largely unused precisely because one cannot read nor even listen to music while using them. Indeed, one can do little else but think as one rows...

In retrospect, I realized as I stroked away that day, my successful battle with cancer has been a divine blessing in my life. Like the aquatic creature for which the disease is named, cancer has multiple arms— long, probing appendages that reach into every aspect of one's existence. Marriage, work, friends, family of origin, and social network... everything is affected to some degree. Although cancer is terrifying and destructive, I have learned the hard way that it can also be a catalyst for personal evolution. My relationships with everyone in my life have improved. I empathize with my fellow humans more readily, and I forgive their failings more easily. Perhaps most importantly, I understand that life is short, that our allotted days of human existence are finite, and therefore of immeasurable value.

During the span of my lifetime, Hodgkin Lymphoma has evolved from a near-certain death sentence into a rite of passage. But more than anything else, my battle with it was and always will be inextricably intertwined with my relationship with Andrea. The events of the previous year convinced Andrea and me that we indeed belonged together, that we were meant for each other. The hastiness of our engagement had felt rash and reckless to each of us at various times. But like the hunter that David had taught me to be, I had pounced upon the opportunity to be with Andrea as soon as it appeared. We had accepted as an article of faith that our paths had been meant to unite, and that we would actually get to know each other in further detail after we were married.

A much higher power had seemed to be guiding us. We knew in our hearts that the juxtaposition of our reunion and my sudden illness simply could not be a coincidence. We had come to believe that I had been supernaturally spared a horrible death by car crash in 1975 in order that I might eventually rejoin Andrea, when both of us were finally worthy of the beautiful love we now shared. And therefore, just as a Canceroid counts each living day as a bonus, every sunrise I share with Andrea seems like part of a joyful honeymoon. I thank God daily for the additional time I have been granted— both in 1975 and in 2008— to enjoy her wonderful companionship.

And finally, as a fully initiated Canceroid I realize that my battle with cancer has not truly ended... nor, really, will it ever. I have learned enough about cancer during the past year to understand that my tussle has ended not with a clear-cut, unconditional victory, but rather a truce. If I manage to keep my cholesterol under control and avoid car accidents and lightning, I may live long enough for this truce to be broken someday. In the meantime there will be periodic tests, CT-scans, PET-scans, and such to detect its eventual return, and medical science will be prepared to face it with ever-increasing efficacy.

But no matter how advanced our medicine becomes, one must accept that no one ever gets off of this ride alive. We are all going to die. There is nothing like falling in love— or the whiff of mortality that accompanies cancer— to highlight the pricelessness of life. In 2008 I was simultaneously graced with both. Thanks to cancer and Andrea, I shall spend the rest of my life cherishing every single one of my uncountable yet finite days.

EPILOGUE

"If God said, 'Rumi, pay homage to everything
That has helped you enter My arms,'
There would not be ONE experience of my life, not one thought,
Not one feeling, not any act, I would not bow to."

Jalaludin Rumi (1207-1273)

* * * * * * * * *

My battle against cancer was over… for the time being, anyway. And perhaps I should say OUR battle with cancer, for indeed it had felt like a collective effort. I owe an immeasurable debt to my team of doctors and medical personnel, my supportive family, friends, and co-workers, and especially Andrea. Our victory has apparently come at the expense of my ergometer-racing career, such as it was… not a bad deal, all in all. Meanwhile, my medical tests will continue for the rest of my life.

In March of 2009 I underwent a pair of important procedures to determine whether or not there remained any active remnants of my cancerous tissue. Some of the worst news that a cancer patient can receive is that the initial protocol, the best shot at a cure, had failed to work… kind of like your Ace starting pitcher getting shellacked in the first three innings of Game 1, and then handing the ball and a six-run deficit to a journeyman middle reliever in the twilight of his mediocre career. Such "plan B" treatments are usually far harsher and yet offer significantly lower rates of success than the ABVD and radiation regimens that I had endured.

The CT- and PET-scans came back negative, as favorable as they possibly could be. But upon receiving this good news I did not immediately feel like a victor or a "survivor," as if the war were over for good. Rather, I simply felt lucky and thankful, and also changed. Cancer, I knew, had changed me forever, and I would now go about the remainder of my life as a full-fledged member of the "Order."

* * * * * * * * *

I find myself thinking about cancer every day at some point. On some days my mind addresses the topic when a fellow Canceroid seeks out my fellowship. At other times I ponder with awe cancer's incredibly complicated biological mechanisms, their mysteries as deep and confounding as those associated with the creation of the universe itself. In order to actually "beat" cancer, I suspect that Big Science will eventually have to find answers to questions it hasn't yet even considered asking... like, for instance, *why* cancer exists, and *why* it perpetuates itself with such determination. And if cancer were simply a "random genetic defect," as current science seems to describe it, then just *how* could mere happenstance produce an entity capable of outwitting Big Science's best weaponry with such seemingly high intelligence?

This "random defect" thesis seems to me to defy probability, common sense, and even the second law of thermodynamics. Such an entity as cancer seems to me instead to be a product of "intelligent design." And if so, then did the same intelligent designer also intentionally grace us with the Yew tree and Madagascar periwinkle, as if playfully hiding such cancer-curing medicinal flora right beneath our noses, like clues to a larger puzzle?

And speaking of "intelligent design," was my cancer perhaps a message from heaven of some sort? In my life I have found convincing evidence of God in everything from a verdant springtime meadow to a glass of heart-meltingly beautiful Pinot Noir. How could the intricate timing of my health insurance, my reunion with Andrea, and my cancer possibly be the product of mere coincidence? It seemed clear to me that a higher power of some sort was orchestrating all of this... to some divine end not mine to comprehend.

192

A Carmelite monk, Brother Lawrence of the Resurrection (1614-1691) once put it like this—

"The worldly people suffer as people of the world do, and not as Christians. They regard sickness as an affliction of nature and not as a gift from God; viewed in this light they find in it only the hardness and rigor of nature. But those who look upon sickness as coming from God, as a consequence of His mercy and as a means he employs for their salvation, ordinarily bear it with great contentment and solace."

* * * * * * * * *

Although I have a somewhat scientific mind and educational background, my aversion to blood, pain, and live innards had always dissuaded me from the study of biology. During the course of my cancer treatments, however, I took an active interest in the biochemistry of medicine, particularly in the poisonous yet curative preparations administered by my oncologist.

The plant kingdom, as I have come to understand it, provides mankind with healing potions for all manner of ailments. That being said, it seems very unlikely to me that a simple and universal cancer "cure" will ever be found among the annals of folk medicine, or beneath a cabbage leaf, or in the herbal section of a New Age crystal shop. And so whenever I read about a "miracle cure" that Big Science or Big whatever is suppressing, the needle on my bullshit meter immediately jumps to the right because I believe so strongly in the Scientific Method. The *"Daubert* test" for acceptable courtroom science is a useful filter for barring unfounded science from the courtroom; and, by extension, for keeping fraudulent and unproven medicine from the marketplace.

However, we have seen that *Daubert* is a two-edged sword, that its rigid requirements can be a legal roadblock to meaningful statistical evidence of cancer-causing chemical products. I find this troubling... after all, neither Adolph Hitler nor Post-WWII scientists needed to know exactly *how* smoking caused lung cancer in order to infer a meaningful cause-and-effect relationship. However, tobacco company lawyers were able to successfully argue for decades against their clients' culpability because of the absence of a known causal mechanism. One might well note that today's physicists aren't much closer to understanding gravity's underlying mechanism than was Galileo, and yet we wholly accept gravity's existence and the precise measure of its influence on massive bodies.

Epidemiology will surely play an important role in future cancer research. More importantly, by the very nature of this particular sub-science, epidemiologists are in a position to identify and recommend relatively inexpensive lifestyle changes that may decrease significantly one's odds of getting cancer.

Since the establishment of the National Cancer Institute in 1937, Big Science has been preoccupied with outwitting and outfighting cancer upon the human battlefield. The diagnostic and therapeutic weaponry has become exponentially more complex over the past seven decades, and correspondingly so expensive that our society's medical reach has surpassed society's capacity to pay for it. In more concrete terms, we have the technology in place to annually screen every man, woman, and child for dozens of types of cancer, and yet the collective medical bill would be impossible for either our government or its citizens to cover.

In contrast, epidemiologists are making it appear both possible and cost-effective to attack the *likelihood of getting cancer* by consuming a healthier diet, one that is more conducive to cancer prevention than the over-processed, chemical-laced fare ingested by most Americans on a daily basis. There are entire bookstore shelves dedicated to their detailed findings, and I therefore refrain here from attempting to summarize their body of work in just a few paragraphs. In general, however, their delineations of foodstuffs to be either sought or avoided differ little from those suggested by Dr. Thomas Hodgkin back in the early 1800's, or Satchel Paige's admonitions about foods that "angry up the blood." A lot of what epidemiologists suggest resonates as common sense.

After scouring a few of these books for information about alleged "cancer-fighting foods," I have come up with a menu to share. Here is a delicious way to get your Omega-3's, antioxidants, and such with a gourmet meal that I dare say might even meet Chef Michael's stratospheric standards.

An Epidemiologically-Correct Anti-Cancer Feast

Wild Alaskan King Salmon Fillet (skin-on, 6-7 ounces per serving)
Salmon is a fatty fish, especially rich in the kind of fat that is good for us. If wild salmon is out of season, look for high quality, naturally raised— yes, *farmed*— Atlantic salmon from a reliable source, such as Loch Duart® from Scotland.

Whether wild or farmed, I have found through experimentation a fool-proof way to cook salmon— preheat your oven to 425°. Cover a small baking sheet with foil. Place fillets skin side down on the foil and smear with canola oil mixed, if desired, with a dab of Dijon mustard. Roast for 10-14 minutes depending upon the thickness of the fillets and the preferred degree of doneness. (Salmon is frequently enjoyed in fine restaurants cooked only to medium-rare.)

When cooked as desired, the skin will conveniently adhere to the foil as you remove the fillets. I like to serve them with a quickly prepared salsa of extra virgin olive oil, finely chopped cucumber, lemon juice and zest, dill, and capers. Alternatively, try topping them with sautéed shiitake mushrooms.

Shiitake Mushrooms
The shiitake is my favorite fungi— silky-rich, and, if you believe the latest nutritional gossip, laden with cancer-fighting compounds. Unfortunately, the shiitake mushroom was a collateral casualty of American cuisine's Great Mediterranean Takeover, surpassed in popularity by the now ubiquitous portobello. But shiitakes are still widely available. Slice them into thin strips and gently sauté them with butter or canola oil.

Organically-Raised Broccoli
I like to cook this favorite vegetable of mine in two steps. First, cut the heads into individual *fleurettes* and blanch them in lightly salted boiling

water flavored with slices of garlic for one minute or less. Immediately strain out the broccoli pieces and plunge them into a large pot of very cold water. Then, after drying them thoroughly and slicing them into thin cross-sections, stir-fry them until lightly browned. Season as desired.

Sweet Potatoes
If one considers starch an indispensable component of the dinner plate, why not a vitamin-rich, complex-carbohydrate-laden tuber? They mash nicely, and I have found that slowly oven-roasting bite-sized pieces of sweet potato with a splash of canola oil also works well. Either way, season with minced garlic (either raw or lightly cooked) and turmeric.

Pinot Noir
Red wine with fish? Lighten up. As an experienced wine professional, I am qualified to assert that the old food and wine rules are… well, old. Drink wine you like with food you like— ideally with guests whose company you cherish— and you'll be fine.

Pinot Noir offers a bright, fresh flavor profile and relatively light body that pairs well with salmon. Furthermore, no other wine provides such a rush of sensual stimulation as a silky and delicious Pinot Noir. If you want to put this meal over the top, look for a biodynamic bottling from France or California.

Dessert?
Yes! Dark chocolate, of course, in one form or another. And have some nice fresh blueberries on the side, along with a cup of green or white tea.

Will a meal like this prevent or help cure cancer? No one can responsibly say with any degree of certainty at this point. However, given none of us will live forever no matter what we eat, there is something to be said for eating food that is both delicious *and* supposedly healthy. Life is short in some cases, but finite always. Given Mother Nature's sprawling smorgasbord of edible delights, why would anyone knowingly opt for a last meal of steamed tofu and kale? Healthy food need not taste punitive.

* * * * * * * * *

We are occasionally reminded by heavenly forces to be careful about what one prays or wishes for. In April of 2009, Andrea and I received the sad news that one of our Wayne Central classmates had perished after his long bout with sarcoidosis. It was quite sobering to recall that I had actually hoped at one time to be Arnie L.'s fellow sarcoidosis patient rather than a Canceroid.

A year after discovering my lump and naïvely hoping that it was sarcoidosis, I was alive... resoundingly, vibrantly alive, and yet a fully ordained member of the Order. As for my fellow Canceroids and some of the other people in my story, here is where they stand as I go to press—

My mother is still actively working as a nurse practitioner while my siblings and I ponder plans for her eightieth birthday celebration. She has no plans to retire from the work she loves.

Four decades after first learning of her illness, Barbara F. remains cancer-free, though she bears the internal scars commonly associated with the harshness of yesteryear's relatively primitive radio-therapeutic oncology. Sadly, her husband perished suddenly in February of 2010, barely a month after being diagnosed with pancreatic cancer.

Janit S. remains an athletic phenomenon well into her forties, setting world-class rowing standards for women her age on the ergometer as well as on the water. She is also a mother of three, which would have been impossible had she opted for chemotherapy instead of radiation. (Prior to her first zap of radiation, a deft surgical maneuver temporarily tucked her ovaries safely out of the radiation's path and thus preserved her ability to have the children she had always wanted.)

Like Janit, my neighbor Kathy R. is a healthy and busy working mother. She publishes a magazine devoted to providing her Berkshire neighbors with information about alternative and holistic healing, organic food sources, and green living.

Dollar for dollar, few retirees enjoy their post-professional years as do former high school teachers. Retired history instructor Al V. is rarely seen without his easy smile and twinkling eyes. Al splits his time between

Florida, world travel, and his wooded acreage in Columbia County, where he generously allows me to hunt for deer.

After winning thirty-eight of his forty-eight games at the helm of the Williams College Ephs, Coach Michael Whalen announced in early 2010 that he would be returning to his alma mater (and Williams rival) Wesleyan College to assume the twin positions of Head Football Coach and Assistant Athletic Director.

Maestro Ronald Feldman, meanwhile, remains at Williams as an artist-in-residence while also directing the Berkshire Symphony Orchestra. Maestro Julian Kuerti is nearing the completion of his three-year assistant conductorship with the Boston Symphony Orchestra. He finds himself in high demand as a guest conductor for orchestras around the world as he weighs his next career move.

I am often reminded that change is a constant in the food and wine trade. Richard Olsen-Harbich continues to bottle some of the finest wines in the northeastern United States, albeit at a different winery. He recently uprooted and now utilizes his talent and experience at Bedell Cellars, just a few miles down Route 25 from his former perch at Raphael. And after many successful years at the stove, Chef Michael has traded his toque for a tuxedo. He now employs his vast body of culinary expertise as a waiter in an upscale Atlanta restaurant.

Judge Loren Brown is semi-retired, but loves the law too much to completely surrender its practice as he approaches his eightieth birthday. To this day he remains emotionally tormented by the consequences of the case of Joseph H., even though his decision not only survived appellate review but also has become a cornerstone of New York family case law.

As we chatted in his Saratoga law office in the summer of 2009, a nominally similar case was making headlines— a Minnesota judge had issued an arrest warrant for the mother of a thirteen year-old boy who had been diagnosed with Hodgkin Lymphoma. In direct defiance of a previous court order, his parents were seeking "alternative medicines," citing religious reasons. "No, it isn't really a similar situation," the judge patiently explained; rather, it was a fairly clear-cut case. The Minnesota parents had defied *existing* family law, a body of statutes that had evolved considerably during the three decades since Judge Brown was compelled to render his gut-wrenching decision.

Anna O. miraculously remains several steps ahead of her cancer as she crusades for research funding between her treatments and hospitalizations. Our 2009 ergometer raffle raised $1200 for "Anna's Hope," her neuroblastoma research charity.

Although the passage of time has been somewhat soothing, Robin T.'s family remains painfully scarred by the 2007 death of their third-oldest child. As more of Ben's surviving siblings marry, there will be an increasing number of grandchildren for Robin to host for their joyous holidays, and yet there will probably always be what feels like an empty chair at their dining table.

Directly across the Spencertown country road from Robin T.'s home, June B. maintains her usual frenetic pace, dividing her time between teaching, travel, and doting on an array of grandchildren ranging in age from one to thirty-five.

In the early spring of 2009 I had the chance to speak with Norma, a fellow Lenox Fitness Center member and the recently widowed spouse of Old Sam. In late 2008 he had suddenly died— not from the cancer that had hounded him for two decades and finally had him treed, but rather from falling and hitting his head hard enough to break his neck. Tragic as this was, I couldn't help but feel a little happy for Sam... try as it did, cancer itself had failed to defeat him. "Don't you see?" I said to Norma, "Cancer thought it finally had him, and yet Sam wouldn't give cancer the satisfaction of taking him down... this was his way of beating it!" Although I have learned to be careful what I wish for, I must confess that I admire the way the old guy left this world.

As I sat with Ann M. during one of her chemo infusions, she glowingly described her renewed relationship with her daughter as a silver lining that had accompanied her pancreatic cancer. It was most fitting, then, that Ann survived her series of increasingly troublesome medical complications to make it nearly through one last Mother's Day.

Throughout her life, Ann had clung tightly to her Catholic faith… and so too at her moment of death, clutching in her fingers an imaginary rosary as she soundlessly mouthed her final "Hail, Mary" before peacefully passing that Sunday evening in May of 2009 with her daughter close by her side.

* * * * * * * * *

In deference to literary economy I have neglected to give my actual employer his proper credit. From 2006 through 2009 I worked beneath the roof of Guido's Fresh Marketplace, but I was actually employed by Mazzeo's Meat & Seafood, an independent purveyor within Guido's' walls. Michael Mazzeo, already as generous and big-hearted as one might ever expect of a boss, took extraordinary pains to make sure that my medical expenses were always covered and that my work schedule never conflicted with my treatments. He even personally donated the shrimp and some other goodies for our wedding reception. I doubt that I will ever have another boss like him.

It occasionally occurs to me that in discussing my cancer treatments I have also given short shrift to surgery in general and Dr. Ari Namon in particular. Surgery was the first anti-cancer therapy, practiced by the ancient Egyptians and thus pre-dating radiation and chemotherapy by two millennia. Although I was spared extensive scalpelry, surgery remains an important modality in present day cancer treatment, in many cases the primary means of treating a malignancy. My surgeon, Dr. Ari Namon, performs all manner of surgical procedures upon the human ear, nose, and throat. In doing so, he is frequently called upon to do battle with cancer— sometimes as the Ace, at other times the Closer, and sometimes as a middle reliever or the set-up man.

And finally, while I have finished my treatments and we now live far away from the Berkshires, Dr. Michael DeLeo and Dr. Wade Gebara, along with their colleagues and staff at Berkshire Hematology & Oncology and Berkshire Radiological Associates, continue to chalk up successful innings against the most vexing illness ever faced by mankind.

* * * * * * * * *

Made in the USA
Charleston, SC
19 October 2010